Anxiety in Relationships

Steps of Therapy for improving Relationship,
a guided conversation to reconnect
couples and to resolve
their conflicts through communication practice
Author Sarah White

of inattention or otherwise, by any usage or abuse of any policies, processes, or directions contained within is the solitary and utter responsibility of the recipient reader. Under no circumstances will any legal responsibility or blame be held against the publisher for any reparation, damages, or monetary loss due to the information herein, either directly or indirectly.

Respective authors own all copyrights not held by the publisher.

The information herein is offered for informational purposes solely, and is universal as so. The presentation of the information is without contract or any type of guarantee assurance.

The trademarks that are used are without any consent, and the publication of the trademark is without permission or backing by the trademark owner. All trademarks and brands within this book are for clarifying purposes only and are the owned by the owners themselves, not affiliated with this document.

4 Anxiety in Relationship

Table of Contents

Introduction

Anxiety can be defined as a natural stress reaction, depending on the reaction levels, can be helpful or destructive. It ensures that anxiety is not harmful as it encourages one to cope with stressful circumstances.

Depression is a psychiatric disorder that is able to express itself in different disorders. For the most part, possible manifestations of depression are a diligent and frustrated state of mind, a limitation of appetite and thinking, lack of intrigue, and a range of physical symptoms varying from a sleeping illness to a craving problem and challenging circumstances.

Depression may be triggered by one element or a multitude of variables. Since each person is different, what drives him/her and induces depression is also different.

Not all, though, feels acceptable amounts of fear as the environment surrounding them causes their nervous responses. Instead, some individuals experience extreme and overwhelming reactions that effectively hijack their minds and prevent them from working their way through their anxious experiences rationally or fairly.

The natural signs of your distress tend to escalate dramatically when you start feeling psychiatric anxiety. Your symptoms tend to become unmanageable and to debilitate instead of only feeling a heightened yet manageable sense of anxiety.

It is suspected that individuals who have anxiety disorder have an overactive fight or flight reflex, which may induce excessive reactions to their initial stimulus or stressor. For starters, if they are dealing with an anxiety disorder, the thought of taking a bus by themselves through the city they've lived in all their lives can cause a full-blown panic attack.

Alternatively, extreme symptoms of pain and tension such as anxiety, elevated blood pressure, and intrusive thinking could be triggered by the prospect of moving to a busy public location. Panic attacks, but also how severe the nervous reaction to a cause is and how quick (or not) it is for the individual struggling to recover control of their symptoms, are not always defined by an anxiety disorder.

The understanding of why fear occurs this way in some persons is not well known, but there are several explanations why anxiety is faced by certain individuals.

For example, whether an individual experienced anything that has become especially painful or upsetting, anxiety can be triggered by their nervous reaction to stimuli that activate the recollection of such difficult experiences. PTSD may also be activated by this sort of stimulus, but it is important that if this is what caused fear, you are aware as to if it is real distress that is being dealt with or if it has advanced to PTSD.

Consistent vulnerability to stress and pressure is often considered to trigger fear in individuals and may intensify with time to problematic distress if they are unable to calm their minds.

This is likely to result through consistent cortisol and adrenaline exposure, which are the two hormones responsible for producing symptoms of tension and anxiety in persons who encounter them. Alternatively, living in a tense relationship with another may often lead someone to feel fear while their abuser can train them all the time to live "on edge." This fear is used to help the attacker who depends on their client to feel nervous all the time so that, without making the anxious victim battle back, they can quickly swing them off balance and exploit them more.

There are genuinely several explanations why an individual can develop anxiety, but problematic anxiety may be troubling and difficult to fend off regardless of how it has evolved. More than 40 million persons globally are estimated to be dealing with anxiety. Living with anxiety can be life-changing, and once it gets debilitating or out of reach, it can have detrimental effects in almost any aspect of your life. For that purpose, it is important for those struggling with anxiety to obtain assistance in coping with their symptoms in order to eventually be healed and resume enjoying a regular life.

11 Anxiety in Relationship

Chapter 01: Anxiety, Negativity and Jealousy in a Relationship

This chapter will introduce you to the aspects which are damaging for the relationship. It also explains the difference between three of them and their possible solutions to overcome them or avoid them completely.

1.1 Anxiety

You are partnering with a great human whom you love. You have built up trust, established limits, and learned modes of communication from each other. Around the same time, you will find yourself continuously questioning yourself, your companion, and your relationship. Would things last long? How do you decide if he's the best person for you? What if they cover up a dirty secret? And if you can't maintain a stable, dedicated partnership, actually? The deep worry has a name for itself: anxiety about relationships. This applies to certain feelings of anxiety, ambiguity, and skepticism that may occur in a relationship, even though all is going relatively well.

Is it normal?

Relationship uncertainty is atypically natural. Some people develop relationship anxiety at the outset of a partnership until they realize that their spouse has similar values in them. Yet, they may be uncertain whether they really want a relationship. And these emotions can often occur in long-term committed relationships. Over time, concern regarding relationships will result in:

- Emotional distress
- Energy deprivation
- Depression or mental exhaustion
- Stomach discomfort and other physical symptoms

The fear is not triggered by something in the relationship. And, in the end, it will contribute to acts that trigger complications and distress for you and your family.

What are some signs of relationship anxiety?

Relationship anxiety will come up in many forms.

At some point, many people feel a little uncertain about their relationship, especially in the early stages of dating and making a commitment. It's not unusual, so you don't typically have to think about passing worries or concerns, particularly if they don't bother you too much. And these tense feelings also spread and float through the everyday life.

Here's a look at some possible symptoms of anxiety regarding a relationship:

Wondering if you matter to your partner

"The most common type of relationship anxiety involves the essential concerns of 'Do I matter? Or are you going to be there for me?' It relates to a simple desire for bonding, belonging and feeling secure in a partnership." For example, you may be worrying that:

- Your spouse wouldn't notice you that much if you weren't around

- They may not be offering help or support if anything negative comes up
- They only want to be with you because of what you can do for them.

Doubting your partner's feelings for you

You've expressed that I love you (or maybe I, really, like you). They are always happy when they come to see you and making nice gestures, like getting you lunch or going out of their way to see you around.

Yet the nagging doubt cannot always be shaken: "They don't really appreciate me." Or they're reluctant to react to physical affection. And, for a few hours, they don't answer texts — even a day. You wonder if their feelings changed because, unexpectedly, they appear a little detached.

From time to time everyone thinks that way, but if you have questions regarding partnerships these feelings might become an obsession.

Worrying they want to break up

A healthy relationship should make you feel affectionate, secure and satisfied. It's completely normal to want to cling on to these emotions and assume nothing can happen to ruin the relationship.

Sometimes, though, such emotions will become a relentless anxiety that your companion will leave you.

This fear will become disturbing as you alter your acts to ensure their continued affection.

For example, you might:

- Avoid discussing problems that are important to you in a partnership, such as persistent lateness
- Ignore while your companion is doing something that annoys you, such as wearing shoes inside your home
- Stress about being angry at you, even though they don't appear upset.

Doubting long-term compatibility

Anxiety about relationships will lead you to wonder that you are completely comfortable with your spouse, even if the relationship is going well. You may also inquire whether you're satisfied or whether you just look good.

In reaction, you may start concentrating your mind on small differences — they love punk music, but you are more of a folk-rock person — and overemphasizing their significance. **Sabotaging the relationship**

Sabotaging behaviors can cause anxiety in the relationship.

Signs of sabotage

Examples of things that could sabotage a relationship include:

- Setting up disputes with your partner
- pushing them away by claiming that nothing is wrong when you are in stress
- Challenging partnership expectations, such as sharing lunch with an ex without informing your spouse You do not do these actions intentionally, but the ultimate objective — whether you know it or not — is usually to know how much your spouse cares.

You might conclude, for example, that denying your efforts to push them away implies that they truly endorse you.

This is very tough for the partner to pick up on the underlying intent.

Reading into their words and actions

A propensity to overthink the partner's words and actions may often reflect concern regarding relationships.

They might not want to grasp onto their hands. And, as you take the leap and move in together, they rely on holding all their outdated furniture.

Indeed, they may all be signs of future issues. Yet they are more likely to have sweaty palms or even like the well-set living room.

Missing out on the good times

Still not sure whether you battle with relationship anxiety?

Take a step back and ask yourself: "Spend more time worrying about this partnership than loving the relationship? Would this be the case in tough times? Because if you sound that way more often than not, you'll definitely be dealing with some anxiety towards relationships.

What causes it?

It can take time to realize what's underlying your anxiety and dedicated self-exploration because there isn't just one clear cause. You can also consider it challenging to self-recognize potential causes.

"You do not recognize a source of anxiety, but regardless of how it is presented, the root causes are generally a need for interaction." Here are several important factors that may play a role:

Previous relationship experiences

You may tend to be affected by memories of things that have occurred in the past when you believe you've gotten through them absolutely.

You might be more prone to develop relationship anxiety if a previous spouse:

- betrayed you
- Unexpectedly abandoned you
- lied regarding their feelings towards you
- exploited you about the nature of your relationship.

It's not unusual to have problems having trust in someone again when you've been hurt — particularly though the new relationship doesn't exhibit any symptoms of manipulation or dishonesty.

Any trigger, whether you know it or not, will also remind you of the past and trigger doubts and insecurities.

Low self-esteem

Low self-esteem may also contribute to relationship instability and anxiety.

Some older research suggests that people with lower self-esteem are more prone to question their partner's feelings while experiencing self-doubt. This will happen as a type of projection.

In other terms, feeling insecure in yourself can make things harder for you to accept that you feel likewise about your partner.

By contrast, people with greater self-esteem tended to help themselves while they encountered selfdoubt by their partnership.

Attachment style

The attachment style you establish during childhood may have a major impact on our adult relationships.

If your parent or caregiver actively answered your concerns and gave affection and encouragement, you've already developed a healthy type of attachment.

If they have not fulfilled your needs regularly or encouraged you to develop individually, then your attachment style will be less secure.

Insecure attachment types can relate in a variety of ways to anxiety regarding relationships:

- Resisting attachment can lead to anxiety about the degree of commitment you create or intensify intimacy.
- Anxious attachment, on the other side, will also contribute to fears that your companion may unexpectedly leave you.

Bear in mind that getting an insecure personality style does not imply you're destined to still feel anxious for relationships.

Because you can't move your relationship style from one form of personality to another, then you can't totally alter it, so ideally, you will make enough changes where a dysfunctional sort of commitment won't keep you down in life. **A tendency to question**

A skeptical attitude can be another factor of anxiety regarding relationships.

Until you decide on a path you might need to remind yourself for all possible interpersonal consequences. And maybe you're already getting used to taking every decision carefully.

When you decide to ask yourself some questions regarding your choices, you would possibly spend some time challenging your relationship, too, long after you have made them. This isn't always a problem. In fact it is usually safer to take time to reflect about choices you made, particularly significant ones (like romantic engagement).

But, if you find yourself stuck in a constant loop of confusion and self-doubt that does not go forward somewhere, it may become a problem.

When one or both individuals in the relationship invest most energy thinking about the relationship than going into the relationship itself." "Fear of rejection, feeling as if they matter most, incessant fear of infidelity, or a general mistrust of the relationship's continuity leads to a loss of faith.

There are many factors you might be worried regarding the relationship; two manipulative spouses set the stage early on in adult life for future issues. Emotional relationships are also used as threats to parents, violent exes, inadequate communication and unsuccessful counseling. Of starters, self-help books on relationships may often encourage elusive, distant, and unexplained acts in holding a spouse hooked. "None of these issues promote a stable, reliable partnership." A person with insecurity regarding partnerships doesn't inherently have an untrustworthy spouse. If you don't express your worries and expectations, your significant companion can well simply live their life, totally oblivious of your problems. Any conduct that allows one spouse to distrust the other at the same time generates conflict. Relationship problems blow up when compared to posts on social media. "The game of competition and contrast fosters insecurity that your partnership isn't as successful as some, which allows pessimistic thoughts to develop when you ruminate that your relationship isn't as 'healthy' as others." That's, of course, just speculation.

Relationship anxiety is a two-person problem

If you have anxiety about relationships, it will definitely be your first impulse to cover it up — especially if you know that your fears are actually overblown. Above all, no-one needs to behave intensely for no reason, or appears to be overbearing. Yet this is the interesting thing about anxiety: while it is often experienced solely by one person in the relationship, it is the concern of both spouses.

If you're an anxious partner, your task is to discuss as quickly as possible about what's bothering you, and why. Does the apprehension find its origins in the baggage of the past? The anxious person needs to be able to accurately perceive the concerns. You don't feel like you've been desired, needed, appreciated or have been the only one? Is the connection lacking an emotionally intimate bond? Is the connection lacking a physically intimate contact? That is when a companion of an individual falls short. Anxiety can be challenging to place in words; it sounds disordered, frenzied and disturbed.

When you are ever unsure about the relationship, here is the formula: Discover the source of the anxiety, explain the trigger to your partner and suggest a fix. "When a partner understands where the anxiety originates, it's easier to come to terms about. On top of this, there would be no dilemma without a solution. Ask them when you think you'd be happier. You may need reassurance, and you may like them to be less vigilant with how they're writing. Giving your partner insight into your feelings. Whether you're not worried because your spouse does, you will probably benefit from it. That includes listening carefully, asking questions, always being honest, and speaking more often than you might find necessary.

1.2 Negativity

Negativity may also come in the form of cynicism, critique, moaning, bullying, pessimism, deceit, perfectionism, and hyper-intensity. Any of these practices will scare away people, including your spouse.

Dr. John Gottman, the creator of The Gottman Institute, who has been conducting relationship research since the 1970s, pointed out that there is a "magic relationship ratio" between negative and positive reactions. In an article about Gottman's results, Kyle Benson writes: "The 'good ratio' is 5 to 1. It indicates that there are five stable and effective relationship for every bad encounter during conflict. Will your marriage endure a significant degree of negativity? Can anyone beat a pessimistic life outlook? Those are good questions which are posed by many couples.

Are You Naturally Negative?

If you're nervous about having or leaning on a negative attitude side, then ask yourself the following questions.

- Do you fall into an unpleasant mood quite often? Do you focus on negative or upsetting thoughts?
- Are you dismissive of everyone in your life? Look at incidents and occurrences, from a pessimistic point of view?
- Are You a Perfectionist? When somebody says, "Good morning," do you question what a good thing is?

- Are you eager to say 'no' to your partner or kids, and never say' yes? 'When you respond yes to any of these questions, your pessimistic attitude might potentially impact your relationship.

Change Your Pattern of Negativity

If you're consistently pessimistic, you can change your pessimistic thinking pattern. You need to make this adjustment, though, and nobody can do it for you.

Here are a few more helpful things you should do:

- Eat a balanced diet.
- Carry in some compassion.
- Get enough sleep.
- Willing to forgive oneself and his kin.
- Practice patience.
- Physical Activity.
- Do something every single day to make yourself content. Simply listen to a favorite song, spend time in an artistic project, enjoy an interesting video, or take a bubble bath.

- If you sense a negative reaction flowing into your head, question this. Then try to think of something positive.
- Volunteer, and collaborate with others.
- Keep in contact with fellow optimists.
- Think of things you're really thankful for.
- Praise the partner anytime a good situation occurs, such as effectively finishing a difficult work project.
- Be open to finding professional assistance.

Help Your Negative Spouse

When you are in a relationship with a person who has a negative mind-set, helping them feel comfortable is not your obligation. Yet these are few measures that you should do to make your partner feel more positive:

- Don't take the criticism personally.
- Know the negativity is their dilemma and not yours.

-
- Should not overreact if your companion rejects your supportive bid.

  Spend time with positive people. You would be willing to take some time out from the stress and negativity at home.

- Invite your mate to take a walk or do something fun with you, at least once a week.
- Consider the successful achievements the individual has accomplished.
- Inspire your partner to seek something new.
- Don't dream about saying "Enough!" and changing the topic to anything more optimistic.
- Be open to getting professional support.

Turn the Negative into Positives

Overall, bear in mind Dr. Gottman's advice: build five positives for each negative. Often, it can be a challenge, and there is no ideal relationship or marriage. Yet having fun, being open to dialogue, and loving one another are some of the keys to a happy and safe marriage.

-

Try the best you can to seek to overcome the negativity you feel. Over time, you might be amazed at the impact it has on both of you.

1. Negative energy

You get so tensed, agitated, and frustrated with your partner while you engage in a toxic relationship that you build up negative energy in your body and later leads to absolute hatred towards each other.

Negativity can rob you in all aspects of your life. Negativity destroys you on an intellectual, physical, personal, moral, and intellectual basis. We are expected to deal with this misery, but that form of stress should be a release from your negative partnership.

2. You are not just happy being in the relationship

Another important indication of a negative relationship is you're not just content anymore. We all realize that in any moment of your life, you can't be perfect, but your spouse can always make you better as a whole. He or she can make you feel secure, dedicated, contented, and ready to do anything you want. This is an alert sign that if you are not feeling positive about your mate, you are in a negative relationship.

3. You don't trust your partner

If you don't trust your partner anymore that is a clear indication of a negative relationship. You're in a destructive relationship when you start questioning your partner's behavior and actions.

When your partner just twists the facts if they don't like the way a conversation is going, it's an indicator you're involved in a partnership with a person that isn't trustworthy. It means you are in a toxic partnership with an untrustworthy individual when your spouse accuses someone else for their actions, or any sort of flimsy circumstances, for their liability.

4. You don't communicate effectively

Much as communication is the very essence of a relationship that is healthy and effective, its lack implies that the relationship is destructive, unhealthy, toxic, and is about to perish. You don't speak to each other face to face, even though you are with each other. You prefer the usage of gestures and texts, rather than verbal communication.

You won't be able to interact successfully in a negative relation. That means you don't even have much to say to your partner anymore. If something occurs in life, whether it's an achievement, an accident, or an event and your partner isn't the first one you're discussing everything with- that's a clear indication of a negative relation.

5. You are not connected to each other

If you do not like being in the company of your partner, it is an indication that you are in a negative or toxic relationship. When you're together, but not really together, it's a clear indication of a negative and incompatible relationship. You may be in the same place; however, one of you is reading, or you are on your phone. You may not feel related to another person even though you both sleep together in the same room.

You are always together because you realize that you never actively communicate with each other, rather you do your own thing; instead, that is an indication that you no longer relate to each other. Which indicates you are involved in a destructive relationship.

6. You feel insecure

If you start feeling uncomfortable in a relationship and don't know your place in a relationship, it obviously shows you are in a negative relationship.

You may feel like; you don't know where you stand or contribute to in a relationship. That is, you are feeling insecure, unsure, or anxious about the relationship's future.

When you're beginning to feel insecure and unsure about a relationship, speak to your partner, and explore where the two of you are heading in the relationship. If he or she cannot provide you with a suitable response or explanation, please get back out of the relationship. Such a relationship is negative, toxic, and destructive, split up, and try as much as possible to avoid the relationship.

1.3 Jealousy

Although feeling jealous is something that anyone can relate to, the feeling is often mistaken with envy. Yet the envy and the jealousy are very distinct. Envy is a response to something that's lacking and a longing for something someone has. They can envy somebody's good looks, or their lovely home, etc. On the other side, the belief that anyone may try to steal what is yours is jealousy. For example, with an attractive co-worker, your husband is fast buddies, and you might feel jealous of their relationship — and disturbed by it.

In its mildest jealousy, it's called an instinctual response that makes us want to defend what we know is ours. While only being territorial, though, jealous feelings can quickly turn into disruptive acts and lead us to behave in narcissistic and manipulating ways. This may even push one to assume stuff that don't exist, like interpreting a casual interaction as the indication of an adultery or working late as keeping a dark addiction.

Jealousy is either instinctual or not, and it's unproductive. People dealing with manipulative, jealous feelings are often frequently grappling with more profound issues. Uncontrolled jealous acts are typically a sign of one or more of the following:

- insecurity
- fear
- low self-esteem

Either of these three or a combination, will not only express a sense of jealousy in disruptive behavior but may also cause certain issues in a person's life.

What Jealousy Does to Your Relationship

Jealous behavior may destroy a relationship. For best, the jealous spouse becomes insecure and deliberately seeks reassurance that they are the only one and that there is no one to substitute them. Controlling and distrustful attitude, and even physical or emotional aggression, can manifest jealously at its worst.

A jealous partner can seek to control the behavior of their partner, check their locations, or monitor their calls, texts, or emails. Such conduct produces an unhealthy habit of mistrust, which eventually contributes to the deterioration of a relationship.

Trust and respect are the solid foundation of a secure and happy relationship. A person dealing with jealousy cannot trust or display affection for the person he or she is with as an individual or his or her boundaries.

Over time this activity would destroy feelings of love and intimacy that once occurred. It will undoubtedly also cause frequent fights, and one person's ability to assert themselves and their honesty over and over again. This may be comprehensive and preclude the formation of a relationship and the creation of a stable foundation.

How Can You Control It

Management of jealous behavior can be difficult. The root issues never all go down on their own. If jealousy is a regular pattern of behavior that is repeated in relationship after relationship, it may require the guidance of a skilled psychiatrist to both rein in it and offer support to cope with the causes that fuel it.

In a relationship going past jealousy means building faith. One spouse must be confident enough in the other to know that the love and affection they share will deter outside influences from disrupting their partnership, irrespective of the circumstances. It can be difficult when one person becomes insecure and usually struggles with trust.

When you have learned that jealousy is a problem in your relationship, whether you are insecure or your partner, it may be tough for you all. Going above, this will require patience, coordination, and beliefs shift. If it doesn't suit to overcome competitive feelings and behavior, don't ignore finding support.

Jealousy is one of the most prevalent emotions among all feelings. You get jealous anytime you know you're going to lose a relationship you really trust. It often adds to tense and mistrustful behaviors that strike men and women with similar rage. Unfortunately, with age, it does not appear to mellow.

There are two very different forms of jealousy: reactive jealousy and suspicious jealousy; this difference is important since nearly everyone experiences reactive jealousy when one knows that a spouse has been unfaithful. But individuals vary in their tendency to experience suspicious jealousy, in the absence of any direct threat.

Reactive jealousy

Reactive jealousy occurs when a couple, for example, is aware of a possible obstacle or risk to the relationship, when one of the spouses learns that the other person was potentially unfaithful. There is often some sort of jealousy in reaction to a realistic threat.

Suspicious jealousy

While the jealousy is suspicious as the spouse has not misbehaved. No sign is provided that a marital partner has engaged in some actions that may significantly, perhaps even legally, impact the relationship's stability. You sit at a restaurant, for example, and you notice that your companion is smiling at an attractive woman across the way. A victim of suspicious jealousy may interpret such a gesture as a threat to the status of the relationship and may become angry with the partner for flirting with the stranger. This is too frequently the case in books, film, and on television, this form of jealousy is sometimes followed by a slap in the face or two partners arguing over the suspicions.

1. Be honest.

If your partner has a valid cause to be jealous, then it might be time to have a heart-to-heart discussion regarding the future of the relationship.

2. Build self-confidence.

It's crucial to understand that signs of jealousy cannot have much to do with you or your actions. If your partner does not have a legitimate basis for jealousy, the presence of jealous feelings indicates that your partner may suffer from a lack of trust. They may be confused about their own situation in any aspect. Encourage your companion to spend time with relatives and colleagues who believe they are great or learn something new.

3. Gain independence.

There might also be jealousy as couples depend too much on the relationship to determine how they feel regarding themselves and self-worth. Convince them to choose to become more independent from you and the relation. The less competitive, the more they attribute their self-definition to their own achievements and encounters away from the relationship. Envy may be almost as detrimental to relationships as the two types of jealousy.

4. Listen carefully.

Do not disregard your partner's feelings and anxieties. It might not have been convenient for the partner to fess up and express his or her thoughts or doubts. This also makes the person feel powerless and not in control. We have always had times like that. Try to understand, empathize, and, if you may listen. If jealousy arises during the early stages of a relationship you'd like to protect, it's cool to be there to comfort your partner when he or she hits the depths of what's causing those feelings of jealousy. At the same time, the adjustments that need to develop will be coming from inside the person.

5. Seek assistance.

Insecurity may be cured easily as, in reality, it is essentially "cosmetic." (For example, if the female partner says she might be more confident if she shed a few pounds.) Furthermore, other symptoms of jealousy, such as those culminating in aggressive behavior, maybe a symptom of greater distress, and is treated best with the aid of a therapist.

Jealousy tends to destroy the base on which to create stable relationships. It is necessary to remember that, overnight, they will not build stable foundations. That's one significant reality.

Misjudgement that jealousy is a symbol of love is popular.

Jealousy may be a major relationship concern — a survey undertaken by relational therapists found that a third of their clients perceived romantic jealousy as a severe problem. They ought to dissipate the misjudgement that jealousy is a sign of love. Yet if not, what motivates these jealous responses then? Studies also associated many characteristics with greater jealousy:

1. Low self-esteem.
2. Neuroticism: a general propensity to be moody, anxious, and emotionally disturbed.
3. Feels low and possessive.
4. Dependence on your mate: Only asking people to consider struggling to find a good substitute relationship contributes to more negative reactions to hypothetical jealousy-causing scenarios.
5. Feelings of inadequacy in your relationship: typically worried your spouse is not going to be good enough.
6. An inappropriate attachment style: a pervasive attitude toward romantic relationships that involves fear that your spouse may or may not value you sufficiently. Research has found that briefly allowing people to feel more strongly connected, by encouraging them to think about

having support from a loved one, makes them react less negatively to a hypothetical, jealousy-inducing situation.

All of these factors which lead to jealousy are about the insecurities of the jealous people, not about the love of their partner for them.

So what do you do when unjustified jealousy is expressed by your mate?

You should be certain that your partner's jealousy isn't about you; it's about them. Respond to jealousy expressions by reassuring your love for your partner. Evidence has found that those who respond by assuring them of their worth and appeal to partners' jealousy tend to have more stable relationships.

What should you do if you're jealous?

How do you deal with jealousy if you are the one who snoops into the emails of your partner? There are some acts that will help you cope:

1. Avoid conditions that could trigger false suspicions. In one analysis, researchers observed that those who were jealous tended to watch their partners' Facebook activities. The

more they sneak in your Facebook or other social media account, the more facts they'd find complaining about, resulting in even greater surveillance and a vicious cycle of intensified control and jealousy.

2. Work in on your own. Concentrate on strengthening self-confidence and relationship.

3. Let your partner know. When you're feeling jealous, speak about it to your spouse — but the way you're communicating about it is key: if you're expressing rage or sarcasm, or hurling accusations at your partner, it won't help. You need to be straight forward but not aggressive. Respectfully clarify your thoughts, and discuss means of finding a solution. It will make you feel more comfortable with your negative behavior and avoid disappointing your partner. These coping strategies are more apt to give the friend supportive reactions.

Jealousy is also justified: because, for example, your wife has an affair and compromised your trust that is a serious issue. When you're upset that you're interacting with someone who doesn't want monogamy when you're doing it, so your insecure emotions might be a legitimate reason to leave the relationship   and   find   someone   that's more   compatible   with   your   desires   for   your relationship. Yet when you get jealous of "stupid stuff," you don't display much love; you reveal your own insecurities.

It tips jealousy over its head. Jealousy is now an opportunity to interact in relationships, rather than one to avoid. Vulnerability is the cradle of love, belonging, happiness, bravery,   empathy   and inspiration. It is where optimism, kindness, accountability and integrity come from. "We will do so in a careful and constructive manner because we recognize that we are jealous. Recognizing and acknowledging the partner's innate flaws and yourself can strengthen the relationship.

Understand your triggers

Jealousy within a relationship may be more about your own flaws than about your mate's actions. Of starters, if you have endured tragedy in your life you may be prone to jealousy. It is important to speak to your spouse about these experiences, because you can be conscious of each other's triggers and accept them.

Jealousy maybe steer by low self-esteem or a negative self-perception. When you do not feel comfortable and secure, it may be challenging to honestly accept that you value your spouse and trust them. Many times the unreasonable expectations may cause jealousy about the relationship. It's not healthy for couples to spend 100 percent of their time together. Remember, the feelings aren't true. Let the pessimistic thoughts float free. Recognize them before expelling them deliberately.

Emotions of jealousy will become problematic if they influence the acts and emotions about the relationship as a whole. Below are some of the signs of sinister jealous behavior.

- Check your spouse's phone or email without authorization
- Insult your spouse
- Presume your spouse isn't attracted to you
- Harass your spouse at their place of residence all day long

- Accuse your spouse of deception without evidence

If you find either of these patterns in your relationship, try and clarify the vulnerabilities.

Use jealousy for good.

Jealousy may also be a very real and rational response to the partner's behavior in a relationship. Remember that people have high expectations for how they are treated in a relationship that is good enough. They look forward to love, compassion, affection, and appreciation. They turn to their mate for fidelity and integrity.

When the reaction is, "Is that so?" "Yeah, so asking your partner how you feel when the jealousy becomes frustration is important. Keep to the" I "phrases as you bring it up and avoid saying stuff like" you do "or" you never. "Talk about your thoughts towards the particular circumstance and making broad conclusions regarding your partner's character. Say what you need and not what you do not. For example, I feel nervous because, when you are out, I don't know where you are or who you are with. I need you to give me update, and let me know. "The better the relationship will be, the more you speak. Is there a specific arrangement that makes you uncomfortable? Do you find that you're stonewalled, or that the spouse's behaviour has changed recently? You and your spouse will be open regarding relationships and working arrangements with each other and out front. "If it hurts, then it reaches a mark. Show each other how much you value each other by placing your relationship ahead of your profession, your colleagues, and your buddies. You develop trust every time you do that. By understanding what controls your feelings, and acknowledging each other's endearing flaws, you will leverage jealousy for the best.

Jealousy is a tangle of thoughts and feelings caused by perceived threats to a relationship, and it gets a bad reputation because of how certain people respond when it reaches them it's harmful if it acts violently, but if it's treated as a force for good it can be a useful signal.

1. Welcome reminder.

The immediate sting of jealousy can prompt you to demonstrate how valuable your partner is to you. "The bond may be complicated by jealousy; we always require a nudge to remember what is really important, so use the feeling as an excuse to simply express the love for your partner.

2. Communication booster.

If you think of it, jealousy tends to reinforce the relationship. "The trick is an effective conversation rather than bottling in the jealousy and letting it come out in unhelpful, passive-aggressive forms – like 'I'm sorry I haven't got a body like that girl who was flirting with you all night at the party. Rather, she advises being assertive and saying something like this," I have to admit you, I've got a little insecure seeing that gorgeous lady flirt with you tonight. You look amazing.

3. Aphrodisiac.

Being riled up at the thought of someone snagging your sweetie may be a potent sign that the physical attraction is either alive — or in control. "It will allow us to see from fresh eyes and rediscover the positive attributes that drew us in the first place," A person we lost confidence in is even more appealing immediately when another woman flirts with him, which can contribute to a precious, revived flame.

You must not wait to act upon such feelings.

4. Goal fuel.

Jealousy causes you to be disappointed with some aspect of yourself, which can be all the motivation you need to take constructive action to change it. For example, "A woman was insecure because of her husband's beautiful and physically healthy coworker. Unhappy with the way she felt in her own body, she was attempting to shed those extra pounds to get the body she needed," the result? It is something the client and her partner will definitely appreciate.

5. Motivation to be a better half.

At times we all get distracted or sluggish, so we might catch ourselves slacking off on our part of the relationship. "Jealousy may be an encouragement to be the greatest partner you can be, but use it to prove how much it means to you. You should surprise him with a meal that you realize he likes or tickets to see his favorite movie. Renewed commitment can" change the relationship and inspire him to become an even better partner.

6. Insecurity radar.

Feeling jealous can lead to deeper hang-ups, so listen to the warning signs and get to the real problem. You can reflect on your "experience with jealousy and realize whether it derives from a feeling of being inferior, whether emerges from adolescence, or you might notice that jealousy comes from a fundamental difference in the relationship, one person becoming far more interested than the other." If so, start thinking about ways you may fix such problems, whether it involves counseling or heart-to-heart with your partner or both of these.

7. Attention tune-up.

It is all too easy for our strained attention to drift away from our most important relationship. No worries – just take notice and take action. "A jealous person found that she was more excited about her children than she was about her husband. To fix this, she purposely offered her husband a huge embrace and kissed anytime she left or returned home. This improved the terms of their relationship.

8. The gift of mutual reassurance.

Think about it this way: When you feel jealous, it is really obvious how satisfying reassurance can be. In other terms, you want your man to tell, "There's nothing to be jealous about. You're everything to me." What you didn't even know is that he feels comfortable because you're honest with your feelings, too. "For him, there is the reassurance that you love sufficiently to be jealous and respect the relationship enough to step up your game. Everyone likes to feel loved and appreciated.

Chapter 02: Irrational Behaviours in Relationship

In this chapter you will learn about the irrational behaviours that comes with the anxiety, negativity and jealousy are discussed briefly and their identification and what to do instead of going after those irrational behaviors.

2.1 A Misunderstanding of Emotions

The concept that women are irrational is always paired with a presumption that logical reasoning is superior to emotion, that rationality contributes to positive choices, and that emotions lead to weak ones. It couldn't be farther from the truth; evidence has demonstrated that it's not just that individuals are not emotionally involved that they don't make smart choices; people can't make decisions without emotions at all. While for effective action, emotions are important.

Philosopher Martha Nussbaum has written of emotions as a means of critical thought, evaluations of the present condition of one's life in the context of one's goals. In this way, optimistic feelings inform us that things are going better for us, and negative emotions inform us that something is wrong in our lives. This awareness provides a critical reference to a successful way of living.

That compares with a traditional perception of emotions as chaotic, stressful, and disruptive; they should be kept under control as such. With this mind-set, often individuals lack the desire to analyze their own or other emotions and therefore have little awareness about their own or other emotional processes. Our society especially deprives men of opportunities for emotional expressiveness and understanding.

The word "irrational" is a refusal to acknowledge the reality of another.

Normally, in a case where the individual does not grasp whether this strong emotion is acceptable, what people mean by "irrational" behavior is a display of strong emotion. And just though the listener doesn't grasp the feeling doesn't mean it has no reasonable justification for this. Quite sometimes, the "irrational" word justifies and maintains cynicism, because it implies the action is the product of such an intrinsically deficient or damaged individual that it defies-and does not even deserve-any fair person's consideration.

Romantic relationships are an arena in which emotions run wild, as do relational misunderstandings and subsequent irrationality allegations. Romantic relationships ask for intense feelings because they are attachment relationships. As adolescents, adults focus on comfort, security, and love dependent attachment relationships. Knowing the desires and vulnerability to one another moment to moment is the cornerstone to successful relationships. When one spouse feels endangered for relationship security (e.g., aggressive behavior or indifference), he or she will respond with strong emotion-isolation, anger, sorrow, and disappointment, when experienced and voiced enough vigorously such repeated responses may also appear irrational.

Emotional upheavals are wise indicators of one's course in life, and the status of the most significant relationships. Invalidating another's personal reality by accusing him or her of being "irrational" leads to violating the person's right to self-determination. Buying into a description of oneself as "irrational" invalidates our own subjective reality and lacks the advantages that our emotions have as a guide to living a healthier life.

2.2 The Relationship Scorecard

What Is It?

The "keeping score" phenomenon occurs when someone you're dating goes on to accuse you for previous mistakes. When both partners do that in the relationship, it's what we consider the "relationship scorecard," where the relationship is a contest to see who gets the most messed up over the months or years, and therefore who is more indebted to the other.

You were a jerk at Cynthia's 28th birthday party back in 2010, and it's ruined your life ever since. Why? For what? What's next? So there's not a week goes by where you don't get reminded. But that's fine because the moment you catch your partner sending flirtatious text messages to a co-worker cancels the ability to indulge in some productive jealousy, so it's sort of rational, right? Wrong.

Why It's Toxic?

The Partnership Scorecard is a draining doublewhammy. You're not just focusing on past failures to escape the current issue, but you're accumulating past guilt and resentment to manipulate your spouse into feeling guilty now.

If this continues on long enough, both sides will ultimately spend more of their energy seeking to show that they are less responsible than the other, rather than solving what created the present issue. Individuals waste their entire time trying to be less incorrect with each other than being more accurate with each other.

What to Do Instead?

Deal with problems individually, unless they are legitimately associated. It's obviously a recurrent concern anytime someone cheats habitually. Yet the reality that she embarrassed you in 2010 has nothing to do with each other, so don't bring it up.

It's crucial to remember that by deciding to be with your significant other, you choose to connect around all of their previous actions and behavior. In the end, if you do not embrace those, you do not accept your partner. When you were troubled with things a year ago because you should have dealt with it at that time.

2.3 Dropping "Hints" and Other PassiveAggression
What Is It?

Instead of expressing it directly and clearly, a companion attempts to nudge the other person in the right direction to sort it out. You'll find petty and subtle reasons to piss off your partner instead of revealing what really upsets you, so you'll feel entitled to complain to them.

Why It's Toxic?

As it demonstrates, the two don't openly and clearly communicate. An individual has no excuse to be passive-aggressive if they feel free to express frustration or vulnerability inside a relationship. An individual would never feel the need to drop "hints" if they think they are not being judged or blamed for their honesty.

What to Do Instead?

State your thoughts and desires freely. So make it clear that the other person is not necessarily responsible or entitled to certain emotions so that you would prefer to be helped by them. When they love you, they will be able to give this support almost always.

2.4 Holding the Relationship Hostage

What Is It?

If one person has a specific complaint or concern, he blackmails the other individual by challenging the entire commitment to a relationship. Of starters, if someone feels like you've been cold to them, instead of saying, "I feel like you're cold sometimes," they'll say, "I can't really date somebody who's cold to me."

Why It's Toxic?

Keeping the relationship hostage is emotional blackmail and causes a lot of unnecessary tension. Even the smallest hiccup in the course of the relationship contributes to a potential commitment crisis. It is crucial for both people in a relationship to realize that unpleasant thoughts and feelings can be shared comfortably without it affecting the whole future of the relationship. Without the freedom to be honest, a couple will distort their own thoughts and emotions, contributing to an environment of distrust and exploitation developing.

What to Do Instead?

Getting upset or not liking something in your relationship is okay; that's called being a normal human being. Yet acknowledge that belonging to an individual is not the same thing as always loving an individual. You can be true to anyone, just not like them all. You may be eternally loyal to others, and often they may actually bother or harm you. In the alternative, two partners who can share advice and feedback without judgment or pressure will affirm their long-term devotion to one another.

2.5 Blaming Your Partner for Your Own Emotions

What Is It?

Imagine you're experiencing a rough day, and your companion isn't too compassionate or supportive about it — maybe they've been on the phone all day with other friends out of town, or they've been busy when you've hugged them. You decide to stay at home together and just watch a movie tonight, but your companion is hoping to go out to meet friends.

When your annoyance with your day – and your partner's reaction to it – comes up, you'll catch yourself lashing out because you're too mean and callous towards you. Of course, you have never asked for moral support, and your companion will naturally know how to make you feel better. They should have gotten off the line on the basis of your crappy emotional condition, to ditch their plans.

Why It's Toxic?

Blaming our partners for our feelings is selfish, and a perfect illustration of upholding improperly defined personal boundaries. This will quickly escalate to a co-dependent relationship if you create a trend in which your spouse is still liable for how you feel (and vice versa). It all needs to be planned-just to read a novel or watching television. When someone begins to feel frustrated, your personal concerns go out of the window, and you need to help each other feel comfortable then.

The main problem with the co-dependent traits is that they generate resentment. It is normal because, once in a while, one person gets angry at the other because he/she has had a bad day and is frustrated and needs attention. Even if it's an illusion that one partner's life should still revolve around the other's emotional well-being, it easily becomes very cynical and often manipulative about the partner's emotions and wishes.

What to Do Instead?

Take responsibility for your own feelings, emotions, and expect your spouse will take responsibility for theirs in exchange. There is a small but important gap between your partner being supportive and your partner being committed. It is to make certain sacrifices by intention and not because this is what is required. As long as all people in a relationship become accountable for each other's moods and downswings, it offers them both an opportunity to mask their real emotions and manipulate each other.

2.6 Displays of "Loving" Jealousy

What Is It?

Get pissed off anytime your spouse speaks, hugs, calls, emails, hangs out, or sneezes in the general proximity of another person, and then you carry out your anger on your spouse and try to control their behavior. That often contributes to insane things such as breaking into the email account of the partner, reading their text messages while they are in the shower, or sometimes following them across the town and showing up unannounced.

Why it's Toxic?

It's surprising that certain people view this as a kind of love display, thinking, incorrectly, that if their mate isn't jealous that maybe they don't love them enough.

That is totally insane clownshit. In reality, it is all deceptive and controlling rather than being loving enough. And it creates needless stress and conflict by conveying a message of a loss of trust in the other. Worse yet, it's demeaning. If a woman is reluctant to allow her spouse to be alone with other attractive women, it implies she believes that he is either a) a liar, or b) unable to regulate the impulses of the wife. That is a woman a person doesn't want to be with.

What to Do Instead?

Completely confide in your partner. It is a radical notion, but it is normal to have any jealousy. Yet extreme jealousy and behavioral control are indicators of your own feelings of unworthiness, so you will learn to cope with them and not impose them on others close to you. You're just going to push your companion away, without resolving your jealousy.

2.7 Buying the Solutions to Relationship Problems

What Is It?

If there's a huge problem or concern in a relationship, you're covering it up with the anticipation and positive emotions that come with getting something great or going on a trip somewhere, rather than fixing it.

For sure, a couple were experts at this one. And that never took them far: a big fat divorce and 15 years of barely talking to each other ever since. Afterward, they also claimed independently that the biggest challenge with their union had been to cover up their real problems with material gratification repeatedly.

Why It's Toxic?

Buying things not only brushes the underlying problem under the rug (where it can always reemerge, or worst the next time), but it still establishes a dangerous trend in the relationship. This is not a gender-specific problem but would use the "traditional" gendered scenario as an illustration. Imagine that if a woman gets angry with her husband/boyfriend, by purchasing a present for the woman or taking her to a nice restaurant, the man "solves" the issue. It not only offers the woman tacit inspiration to find more ways to get upset with the man, but it also provides the guy absolute zero incentive to accept complete accountability for the relationship issues. Is that the end of it all? A husband who behaves like an ATM and a wife who is unceasingly cynical and unheard-of woman.

What to Do Instead?

Tackle with the problem. Will it ruin the trust? Think of what it takes to restore. Does anybody feel disregarded, or not appreciated? Speak regarding how to develop an appreciation for those feelings. Communicate!

There is nothing wrong with doing nice things for your partner after a fight to show support, regret, or reaffirm the bond. Yet, one should never use gifts or costly things to avoid dealing with the underlying emotional issues. Gifts and vacations are called luxuries for a justification-you can really enjoy them when everything else is already great. If you try to manipulate these incentives to cover up your problems, you'll find yourself with a much bigger issue down the line.

2.8 Irrational Jealousy

Every single emotion is natural. The emotion isn't itself unreasonable. But how we make choices depending on our feelings may be unreasonable and affect negative behavior. Although many actions linked to the emotions can trigger difficulties, the itself emotion can be justified. The emotions seek to give us with knowledge. When we get the details, we will then opt to take reasonable action. Emotions may, therefore, be mistaken like any details. Whether we make awareness of the emotion can't necessarily takes to the precise nature of an emotion.

Hence, our actions cannot resolve the difficulty given to our attention by the emotion, or might even generate unnecessary difficulties. For starters, let's look at the feeling of agitation. Imagine a situation where an individual has not been invited to a wedding, is exempt from a particular event. In that situation, it would be normal for the individual to get hurt and upset. "Why does she not invite me? I have always been there for her." The anger-providing information then is that the person feels rejected and left out of a significant event. If the individual acknowledges this information, he may decide to respond by confronting his friend and voicing how he feels: "I don't understand why I wasn't included." In this case, he would figure out whether the slight was unintentional or whether there was a reasonable reason, or maybe his friend has an issue with him because she didn't deal with it. This allows him the opportunity to cope with the situation irrespective of what the problem is, and to seek and fix it. What if, however, he misinterprets the anger: "She's always cutting me out. She doesn't really care about me," and in turn, he's assured of rejecting her. Even if, right before her wedding, he decides to write a harsh letter about how ungrateful and inconsiderate she is and give it to her?

The first reaction to the outrage was based on a reasonable and objectively reflective interpretation of the rage. Nonetheless, the second explanation was an erroneous definition which can inflict damage to the relationship beyond restoration. If it gets unreasonable, the emotion of jealousy is represented. Other definitions of the emotion of jealousy may be explored more, and how to determine what the sensation entails. Finally, as it is unreasonable, the origins of excessive jealousy should be investigated, and opportunities to know how to handle jealousy should be concentrated.

What Is Jealousy?

Jealousy has long been seen as obsession and ravaged society. Looking at classic literature, or even the Bible, you'll find endless stories of jealousy and revenge. Throughout the early 1900s, researchers had researched jealousy among college students. One reviewer of this research says, "Jealousy is a fundamental instinct that bears a close resemblance to anger, terror, and sorrow, and demonstrates a correlation to the proprietary instinct. It is a defence against social instinct, and reciprocal help provides a clear antidote to jealousy (Withy, 1907), that is, jealousy is a specific instinct linked to the desire to control, particularly in relationships and that the more people try to help one another rather than compete, the less jealousy is experienced. Jealousy is a loss-based emotion or fear of loss like a relationship or friendship. Other emotions are usually present, such as fear, rage, sorrow, or sadness. The person also experiences negative feelings of fear and thoughts.

While Jealousy and Envy are somewhat similar, they are not considered the same emotion. Jealousy refers to the lack of something that the person already has, while envy is the longing for something that the person doesn't have. However, it can be argued that jealousy and envy can be nearly identical in certain circumstances. For example, if a person has been passed over for promotion, she may feel envious of the co-worker who has earned the promotion. Since she had not lost everything she had already (her job), it would not be called jealousy. We may, however, claim that she has lost something in her hands, such as her sense of adequacy or competence reflected by the promotion. In this case, it may be called jealousy to feel towards the co-worker; hence, while scientific research shows a clear difference between jealousy and envy.

When Is Jealousy A Normal Emotion?

As stated earlier, all of the emotions are natural. Jealousy is even more than a human instinct. Imagine a wife only discovering that her husband is about to leave her to another woman. Of which she would be jealous. In this case, the resentment that she experiences is part of her grief process. Her anger and jealousy are directed against her husband's focus of attention.

And many teenage girls, for example, encounter intense emotions in their friendships, such that if a friend decides to spend more time with another friend, they may feel rejection, frustration, and jealousy. Sadly, if, owing to anger and jealousy, they do not have assistance in establishing methods of solving this problem, they are likely to permanently break the bond. However, this increasing resentment is also a valuable lesson in learning how to build relationships that are emotionally mature. Ultimately, most teenagers understand that the case is not actually a failure and that their friendship hasn't been compromised. We realize there's more than one close friend that a particular individual may have. However, many individuals will not know this lesson, so, therefore, they begin to develop emotionally unstable relationships throughout adult life.

As you can tell from these cases, the general characteristic of natural jealousy is that it diminishes in intensity over time and only persists for a brief period of time. This is valid for most human feelings. Now, the time span may certainly differ depending on the circumstances, but the person will eventually resolve the emotion and move on psychically. Nonetheless, for unreasonable jealousy, the individual can stay stuck in the emotional experience for an indeterminate amount of time. But it can never improve without major reform initiatives.

What Is The Purpose Of Normal Jealousy?

1) Motivation to Improve.

Like every emotion, natural jealousy asks one to take a deeper look at a certain situation, or ourselves. This will make us become more mindful of our own vulnerability so that we can overcome this.

2) Motivation to Resolve a Problem

And, it could warn us that someone treats us in a hurtful way. For starters, each time a woman is out with her husband, he checks out other women and flirts with them. The woman may feel that other women are jealous of her. Yet if she examines the situation, she may be swayed by the jealousy that she's upset that her husband doesn't want to pay attention to her and that he doesn't care about her feelings. This acknowledgment allows her the chance to speak to him about her feelings, and eventually fix the issue.

3) A Warning

Another jealousy purpose might be to warn us of some potential loss. Social connections had to be established throughout human culture in order to thrive. This makes sense in this context for people to foster jealousy as a means of motivating them to defend their resources to increase their likelihood of survival. Jealousy might not be as important for survival as other evolutionary behaviors, but within our social communities, it is still a vibrant force.

When we look at the previous case again, the woman's jealousy may have tried to express the possibility of her spouse abandoning her in terms of warning. However, we need to be careful about this concept because it may quickly trigger unreasonable jealousy without adequate proof. And it might be prudent for her to check her feelings with him, "I'm afraid you may abandon me when you pay so much attention to other women." His response might offer her an indication of this emotional warning's accuracy.

What Is Irrational Jealousy?

Irrational jealousy, also known as morbid jealousy in psychiatric literature, happens when the jealousy is not founded on reality, or where the individual's jealousy appears out of proportion to the situation. Yet the feeling is more than just a flickering one. Usually, the individual not only dwells on the jealousy but also participates in some form of negative behavior.

For example, a man who believes his wife is flirting with any man she talks to when she's only engaged in normal conversation may feel irrational jealousy. He not only constantly asks about her interactions or obsesses over her, but often endlessly questions her about every aspect of her day. For the first time, she will console him and decides not to talk to other men, but learns slowly that there is no reassurance that will fix the circumstance. She's going to become upset and resentful, which might cause what he's scared of — she'll be leaving him.

Another example (although that is more about envy) is someone who focuses obsessively on her neighbours' life and unfairly compares with her neighbor. However, she may also see the neighbor as undeserving of her good fortune, and engage in vicious chatter with other neighbors that is a kind of revenge, the action often associated with jealousy or envy.

What Are The Problematic Behaviors That Occur With Irrational Jealousy?

1) Violence

The conduct that is of great concern is the tendency to perpetrate aggressiveness. It has been commonly reported to have been due to jealousy with the abuse of women. Nevertheless, having clear scientific evidence of the mechanism of rivalry and violence was challenging.

DeSteno et al. (2006) showed that jealousy causes aggression. Seeing that it is difficult to actually generate jealousy and violent acts in the research setting, not many researches has been conducted to find out how jealousy leads to violent acts.

Nevertheless, researchers DeSteno et al. (2006) have established a new method of using hot sauce as a retaliatory instrument and providing the spurned person the ability to impose vengeance on the other without having noticed anyone. As a consequence, they specifically found that the rejected individuals were more likely to attack the person who rejected them.

Researchers have noticed the violence to be focused on a reduction in self-esteem that culminated in heightened jealousy. In other terms, it will be noted that many that have not experienced a decline in self-esteem are unlikely to aggress, nor are those who have experienced a decline in self-esteem and no jealous feelings.

2) Stalking

Stalking is related to the issue of violence, which is an effort to intimidate someone, either by trying to convince the other of his / her loyalty or by more transparent forms of influence. The need for dominance is a core feature of stalking behavior. In fact, the individual may encounter a pattern of emotional connection, with feelings of frustration and jealousy.

3) Retribution

Another kind of aggression is revenge towards another person. Retribution, though, may not have to be an outright aggression; in the context of gossip, it will be more subtle, passive-aggression behavior. In fact, revenge has become too easy these days across social-networking sites as individuals are free to make hurtful remarks about someone who, in previous decades, may have been more private. Retribution often winds up escalating conflicts rather than fixing them. Imagine a situation in which a spouse is irrationally jealous of his wife, has access to their Facebook account, and under her name makes nasty comments regarding her male friends.

4) Obsessive Talking or Questioning

A very common jealousy-related behavior is to continuously think about the issue of jealousy or to vigorously question people to determine if their irrational beliefs are correct. The problem with this interrogation is that there is no way to ensure whether it has not occurred. The questioning instead just persists, as the person is never assured.

5) Distrust

Another outcome of jealousy is distrust, which is an unpleasant situation and not conducive to the development of good relationship growth.

Causes of Irrational Jealousy

1) Fear of Loss

The most noteworthy characteristic of irrational jealousy is the fear of loss. This loss may take many types but generally falls into the definitions of lack of control, loss of self-worth, or loss of self-sense. An individual who perceives his opponent as having a greater financial power may be a lack of control. Ted Turner reported years ago that even the top multibillionaires were hesitant to make big charitable contributions because they were afraid of losing their spot among the wealthiest in the world. He said each of them continue to pay the same amount so that their standing stays the same. Which means they are going to be philanthropists and carry out benevolent acts without sacrificing their power.

And maybe they saw their position as an indication of self-worth in the documents, which is another type of failure that people fear. And lastly, the third type of failure is self-sense. An example of this could be a man who sees himself as the protector of his family and is terrified at sacrificing his wife and kids.

2) Inadequacy

Individuals who feel inferior to someone else or some particular ideal are more likely than others to experience jealousy or envy. Researchers at Northeastern University found that undermined selfesteem is a central contributor to irrational jealousy (DeSteno et al., 2006). Individuals whose selfesteem is based on an external source such as a relationship might be more susceptible to irrational jealousy as protecting existing sources of selfesteem becomes more difficult. Whereas those who concentrate on love and self-acceptance of selfesteem are less prone to loss of self-esteem, and thus less susceptible to jealousy.

3) Fear of Feeling

Although none of us like uncomfortable feelings, many people with extreme jealousy are especially terrified of feeling rejected or frustrated and are taking dramatic measures to try to avoid these feelings. Sadly, their aggressive behavior can create what they want to avoid, as well. Emotional anxiety or sensitization may arise from past experiences such as childhood rejection or a former partner that betrayed them.

4) Delusions

The origin could be based on paranoia in a limited group of individuals with jealousy issues. As such, this implies that the individual can experience a severe psychological disorder such as paranoid schizophrenia. One crucial path to discerning the difference between irrational jealousy and paranoia is for the deluded person to truly accept the truth of the faith. Although an adult with irrational jealousy is more likely to say, "I know I'm wrong, and it creates issues, but I can't help myself — this is how I feel."

5) Obsessions

Obsessions or, even more probable, ObsessiveCompulsive Personality Disorder (OCPD) can be the cause of repeated behaviors in a particular group of individuals. The aforementioned causes of jealousy, such as fear of losing, inadequacy, and fear of feeling, can be reflected in these individuals, but they are bundled in a web of obsessions. Such people, often identified with reality, may have what is known as "overvalued ideation," which means that they might have enhanced difficulty in recognizing the irrationality of their jealous thoughts.

What Can Be Done regarding Irrational Jealousy?

The method to deal with irrational jealousy depends upon the root cause:

1) Mental illness

If the jealousy is psychotic, treating the delusions requires professional assistance and care. Individuals with OCD or OCPD require Cognitive-Behavioral Therapy (CBT), at least, and can even benefit from medication.

2) Inadequacy

The individual has to address self-esteem issues for inadequacy problems. For certain individuals, this is fairly easy, because they recognize the low selfesteem. In this scenario, utilizing the cognitivebehavioral development techniques to question unreasonable thinking may be helpful. For others, that may be more difficult as they do not realize the problems of self-esteem and may be dependent on feeling positive. They might need to do more research to gain a better perspective.

3) Fear of Feeling

People who are taking dramatic measures to avoid feeling miserable will know how to deal with their sorrow. In battling the excessive fear of feelings, we can recover from both grief counseling and CBT. It is likely that they already had previous unresolved grieving instances.

To begin with, a woman may have had a former unfaithful spouse, and now has intense jealousy towards her present spouse, even if he has offered her no reason to be jealous. She was unable to cope adequately with her previous grief, and it is mirrored in her current relationship's jealousy.

4) Fear of Loss

The fear of losing the problem is handled in a manner that is close to the fear of feeling. The main difference is that the feeling of failure is geared into the future, as though the person were grieving something that has not yet happened. This may even find its roots in previous experiences of grief. So the irrational assumptions are to be overcome and understand how to deal with sorrow.

Sometimes, when you meet your someone that responds or behaves very often with a sequence of mere toxic characteristics. So poisonous, you have to be very cautious around them, and they don't strike towards you. They do this due to the reason that they are not stable emotionally.

Victims of Irrational Jealousy

Several victims either lived or they are in a relationship with a psychologically ill adult. These are some of the bad words they used to describe who these toxic individuals were: angry, violent, messy, clingy, whining, irritating, intimidating, offensive, inhuman, dangerous, deceptive, unreasonable, humiliating, difficult, demeaning, futile, destructive, sad, disturbed, disorganized, disturbing, dramatic, chaotic, painful, envious.

While the previous list of words is not a tool for diagnosis and cannot be applied in that manner, it gives us an insight into individuals that have gone through from what life is like and what they are seeing as an emotionally distressed adult. One term or one event does not render a bad personality — everyone has a bad day — if the individual shows a significant amount of actions exhibited in this category on a daily basis, we are seeing someone who is not emotionally stable, and they needed treatment.

Clearly, nobody have all the characteristics. Yet not a lot of people have come across dealing with someone who frequently reveals a variety of things to be jawdropping. Working around anyone like that is "a living nightmare" in the words of some victim. What the perpetrators have depicted becomes an environment where things are routine for one minute, and a violent attack happens for the next. All is perfect for a minute until the moment further, with the smallest warning, there's an verbal assault that can lasts for long time, and leave you terrified, angry, disillusioned and question your own rationality. These individuals are volatile in how they communicate with others, so you do not believe you can trust them — chaos always seems to be right near the edge, a small mistake or away from a misspoken word. You might have to move with caution, for survival, even though on eggshells.

People remain in such relationships out of passion, concern, or desire thinking their new precious gift or kindness act gets things better. This does not. No number of kindness or contrite would ever allow them to adapt.

The person compelled to change becomes the victim, which will have to acknowledge to either "bear it," as suggested by one survivor, or become so hesitant that with this emotionally unstable attitude, they cannot articulate their minds or consider living in the same environment. How people stay in these kinds of relationships is still confusing or a total secret, but one thing is for sure: the dysfunctional person needed help. So, you just can't personally repair them.

The last option you can try is strive to obtain some professional assistance for them, but it may backfire. The psychologically ill sometimes cannot see something bad with them, they dismiss their work, or say that you are a perpetrator, not them, and so they strike at you. But they need help. Professional help through somebody who is worthy of dealing with such individuals. You might also require a competent clinician to help you know that you have no liability for all like this.

When you encounter or are in a relation with anyone like this, be vigilant not to get traumatized. When crime happens, as is always the case, you will find support.

Besides from the above words of the victims, the following can refer to the mentally disturbed individual.

1. The intense show of frustration are somewhat out of proportion to the event or the situation.

2. You became less contented, less hopeful, or less self-confident after you learn or have entered into a relationship with that person.

3. The relation is best defined as "roller coaster" lows and highs.

4. Is incapable of recognizing the implications of his derogatory remarks or acts and how it will have effect on others, also including relatives or community.

5. Behave in circumstances that are often unacceptable or absurd.

6. At each and every time, it appears to fall apart, or get mad at the slightest tension.

7. Arguments of few seconds will continue for days or hours without any effort to change or interrupt them.

8. The smallest incident will lead her/him to get angry and act out.

9. Cases of brawls, fights, or direct confrontations are common.

10. Sometimes for total strangers or even medical providers such as a therapist, verbal altercations or disputes appear to be a part of life.

11. You can't seem to be comfortable, calm, or "holding down" with this person.

12. Those who are close will "check" periodically to see what the current "mood" is.

13. It is defined by some as "unstable" or called for throwing away things or destroying property.

14. Says that they forgive but they never do: mistakes, injustices or failure are specifically remembered for usage in upcoming arguments.

15. One has got a "short temper" and a low degree of frustration.

16. Incapable of sincere empathy, sympathy, or love yet even requiring you or anyone to do so.

17. You often feel afraid to speak or respond from fear of the potential reactions that this

person might have towards you, or that they might injure themselves.

18.   You feel trapped by the person in certain aspects.

19.   Using guilt as a retaliation tactic or puts you down to boost their self-worth.

20.   They also cry out not just with remorse but also with a vengeance. Even appallingly.

And if any of the above words align with you, they can be a person with emotional instability. Although these entities will seek to make it look like that everything is at fault because of you, or that you don't have any sense, that's because they're badly at fault. There might be several bases as to why they are so, but in no way does that justify how they make you feel or treat you. You do need professional care, and it isn't your duty to become the human punching bag of the mentally distressed individual.

Your duty is to separate yourself and your children, if there is need to be, from this sort of character before they give you any harm. Regardless of what people might suggest about you, remind yourself this: "You never have a social obligation to be marginalized." We've all had anyone tell us anything that appears to be completely off the wall and tried to argue with them — trying to convince them to see it our way. Will it work so much like that? The quick answer to this is Never. Never have.

Then, the argument tends to intensify out of control with neither of you responding to the other, and it's usually getting nasty.

When people get upset, the rational mind goes off, and the animal mind takes over. They begin to respond out of panic, triggering their response to fight-or-flight stress responses. And it's like attempting to explain something about someone that speaks a separate language than you, seeking to argue for someone who has separated themselves from their rational brain.

So when someone around us begins responding to us from the place of fear, from the wounded ego, this causes our own responses to fear as well. When that occurs, the sides struggle to respond or negotiate rationally, and the relationship becomes an unreasonable and unproductive thing.

So, what's the alternative?

The alternative is to make your own reaction conscious. Your original thoughts can sound insane like this. That's just not true. That is not real. It is out of the wall. They are imprecise.

In reality, the first goal is to be respectful of these emotions, take a deep breath, and remember that you can't change someone else's beliefs. You don't have much influence over what they're doing, how they're behaving, or whether they're treating you or themselves.

The toughest part of this process is recognizing the insufficient control over others. If you tolerate the failed effort to connect with them in that case, you may opt to take an approach that would help you: either comfort them because they are responsive to you, or walk away and take control of your own feelings.

It can be incredibly difficult. We desire too desperately to convince people to see "the truth," particularly those we care for. We want them to avoid being crazy and reconcile with us. It's scary when the people we worry about quit making sense.

That is why the best way to feel safe is not to slip into the chaos. We give in to the crazy as we try to scream, defend, clarify, yell, etc.

Someone is not present much of the time in an emotionally driven setting or is vulnerable to warmth. When you know that this entity is inaccessible to you in this situation from prior experience, so the only safe and rational choice is to get out of the situation — not with anger or remorse, but with solid, gentle detachment.

It usually takes about 30 minutes for a human's higher brain to come online while stressed and irritated, but wait at least half an hour before seeking to re-engage. You will always search for opportunities to see how the other person is doing.

If they start to settle down, maybe you should speak to them about the situation that prompted them to respond from a wounded position. But it could be easier to just let it go. Experience will show you which benefit is greatest.

It takes bravery not to jump in to try to reassure the other individual to quit "acting nuts." Some of us care too much for preventing the feeling of helplessness over others that we will do almost anything not to accept the reality.

After being disengaged, humbly welcome the feeling of helplessness and let the feeling float into you. It's for sure that you will be empowered because you're able to take proper care of yourself, rather than arguing for someone who can't listen to you or acknowledge you.

Chapter 03: Understanding Each other

This chapter highlights the importance of mutual understanding and all the other aspects that come along with it to understand one another. It is the crucial step towards building a healthy relationship.

3.1 Why is Understanding Important in a Relationship?

There is a fine distinction between understanding and being defensive.

Understanding is where you want to learn and appreciate the reason behind his / her actions, and defending is where you start explaining all their acts only to comfort yourself.

Now on to the issue, why is it important? Think about all sorts of relationships here (friends, families, marriage, professional, etc.) just take an example; He- it's 12 o'clock she has to call me, it is my birthday.

She-let's not call him in the morning. However, I will surprise him in the morning.

Here He got two options either blame her for not calling at 12 o'clock in the morning or just have patience and wait to know the cause.

Another example is; She- He told me he'd never speak about his ex-wife or see her, so why the heck he'd seen her today.

He- She Maybe my ex-wife but she needed support today, I wish that 'she' isn't angry at me.

Whether she should fight here, or she should actually want to understand his point of view.

So, why understanding is important in a relationship? Because

- Two-person can, at the same time, have a separate viewpoint on the same problem.

- The scenario might not be what you perceive appropriate.

- The individual can have several explanations for not reacting to you.

- Everyone deserves a shot.

- Every partnership relies on the perception of one another.

- Value someone else's opposing opinion.

- To want and learn but not explain the purpose of the conduct.

- Knowing that another individual was correct to have a totally different viewpoint than ours.

- To realize that you will always respect each other without feeling the same way, without deciding to anything and without simply obeying each other.

- Know when to say, 'let it be.'

In any relationship, the degree of understanding defines the strength of your relationship.

Everyone wants to be noticed, heard, and understood. We like that from our partners in particular. We want our spouse to tell, "Yeah, I listen. Yeah, I do. Yeah, I understand the pain that you have. I'm sorry that hurts, and here I am. We like our spouses to be involved in what is going on within our heads and to care about it.

The fundamental human desires are the need to be seen, heard, and recognized.

One of the most frequent concerns relationship therapists receive from their clients is that they don't get that from their spouses — even if it's strong and essential to healthy relations. "Feeling noticed, validated, and recognized contributes to greater trust and relational growth." When we don't have that, we feel excluded, and like we don't matter, which may weaken our bond over time.

There is a common (inaccurate) assumption that our spouse's interpretation implies we have to agree with them. However, you might absolutely disagree with that. Rather understanding simply means listening thoroughly and intently to our spouses. It comes down to understanding what they claim. This involves asking your spouse, "I believe I understand you. So let me check: What you're saying is, "That implies sticking through this process" because your companion doesn't need to explain their viewpoint even more since they realize you get it. You really understand it, even though you don't approve.

Below are the suggestions shared on how we can "get it" and better understand our partners.

Be fully present.

You do not need to do something while your spouse is talking. You don't have to try to fix that situation or make things smoother. "The only role is to have the partner express their human experience with another being."

Understand first.

"Make sure to understand first, then be understood. Seek not to compose the responses while the partner is speaking. It also prevents you from digesting what they are saying thoroughly, which impedes genuine comprehension. "They would obviously reciprocate with interest regarding what you think, and experience as your spouse feels heard so you will have a chance to express your viewpoint."

Avoid complaints and defensiveness.

Defensiveness and complaints are characteristics of dysfunctional interactions that keep you from really intimately bonding. When someone criticizes and argues, they put their partner unintentionally on the defensive. It shows your spouse that "it's not me; it's you." "And the key is to accept any accountability, just a little iota, a weensy tidbit — 'I've understood your point, I've agreed I'd ... I've got to ...' It's always good to inform your spouse how you feel about what you need.

Manage your own stuff.

It is important to remember that knowing our spouses always requires recognizing ourselves. It's tough to handle all the material that pops up and sits in the way of actually listening because you've got a lot of emotions and needs prickling at you.

That's why calming down, and spending some time interacting with your own feelings and needs is necessary. When you need to do this, be frank with your partner: "I want to understand you, but first I need to sit by myself, will you give me time? It would sound better than not being heard by your partner.

Pay heed to your bodily sensations to fine-tune your feelings and needs. This lets you consciously understand what is happening to you, and you can then discuss it with your spouse. For example, you may consider: "Does your neck's or arms hair prickle up? Does your heart race? Do you feel flushed? Will you be controlling your pace carefully? What is it that you need to feel calmer, soothed, and safer? "Our appreciation of our partners requires diligence on our side. It demands that we stop and not disturb our companion or try to formulate responses in our heads. It demands that we shift our complete focus to them.

That is not a simple job. So practice is required. Yet it still gives a wonderful gift to our partners: the joy of being accepted for who they are and what they deserve.

Couples get together to believe in the idea of happiness. Couples are sticking together as they really feel they will make things work. People in relationships want pretty much the same things: affection, stability, trust.

There is a way to create a better bond, but there's no way to establish it until you completely grasp your partner's inner feelings and such. You may say to yourself: "I understand my wife, of course. She won't let me forget what I need to know about her. "You may think this is understanding, but it's recognized as ignoring something you're sick of listening about. There's something very different from understanding.

The reason the couples complain about each other is that their desires are not being addressed. Those needs differ with every person. One spouse will feel distant from her husband and may want to feel as though she is important to him. If this were revealed to her husband, he might also be able to do anything to make her feel better. It may sound like, "Honey, I'm glad to be with you." It doesn't take anything to fill in what's needed so long as you know what's required. This is comprehension. Unfortunately, it typically sounds like, when people are upset, "Oh, you didn't pick up the dinner dishes. Why wouldn't you ever take the garbage out? "Such critiques can provide us with an example of the feelings beneath. They can feel neglected and become depressed and then furious, and all those feelings come out of complaints about dinner plates or garbage.

Most of us are not encouraged to explore our inner feelings — those that render us cross with our partners. Then we just take the sorrow and the frustration and turn that into a critique in the expectation that we can at least get something back. Yet, sometimes, the return response becomes worse. Nobody wants to be questioned, and nobody reacts to criticism well. It does hurt. What we find in a lot of marriages is feeling hurt on top of feeling hurt. One party is saying something negative, and the other is replying and putting it on a notch. They still feel betrayed and misunderstood. This might also transform into a habit in which people wind up staying. "It's not that horrible," they might rationalize, but it's not good either.

Many people know how to offer an excuse to overcome hurt feelings. Anything like this could go, "I'm sorry I was rough and said that to you," this helps with bringing the pair back on equal terms, before the next bit of misunderstanding, but most people don't even know how to speak to their spouse about what they want, and they end up feeling upset about it.

It may be useful to know what happens within the individual before the assault begins. That's where understanding plays a part. If she realized she wanted to feel valued and respected by her husband, maybe she should ask for it. This may sound like this, "Honey, sometimes in this partnership, I feel as though I'm isolated, and it doesn't really matter what I do. I realize that's not the case, but could you please let me know I'm important to you right now? "That's not how people communicate in actual life, so it's awesome to know what you need to for your partner to give that to you. This needs feeling comfortable enough to be vulnerable, and this is a point certain people consider this tough to get to. This is exactly the situation where counseling helps.

If spouses were to know in the moment what their spouse requires, wishes, or desires, they would both be able to give that to him or her. Similar people like to see their spouses satisfied. Couples having a healthy partnership don't want their partners hurting. The important thing is getting people to accept each other and themselves in order to feel satisfied. When couples master this, it's easy to find out.

Try to make your partner aware of this. What is it that he likes, needs, or desires? You will be good to be on the way to a stronger relationship when you know this; one with affection, stability and, above all, understanding.

In an intimate partnership, there is an explanation of why understanding is one of the main characteristics of a successful relationship. Apart from the fact that this characteristic encourages your companion to be who they wish to be without being afraid of judgment, it helps you to view it from the perspective of others.

When you're always struggling in a relationship to learn how to be a more compassionate husband or wife, so appreciate and practice these really important features.

3.2 Ways to be more Understanding

There are ways in which a partnership may be more understanding.

1. **Take time to get to know more about your partner.**

The difficulty in attempting to comprehend another person rests in the reluctance of one to genuinely consider them not only as a companion but also as an individual being capable of various emotions and feelings. When you don't know them, it's hard to ever learn how to appreciate someone: their strengths, their joys, their worries, and even their imperfections. You will take your time, as a partner, to get to know your partner better. This may take months or years, but it's all going to be worth this, particularly if you want the partnership to succeed.

2. **Be mindful of your own feelings and motivations.**

It can be daunting to know how to comprehend another human if you don't quite understand yourself. How well do you know one another? What is it that makes you happy, sad, or angry? How can you get inspired by those feelings? How do they help you make choices? If you learn for yourself the answers to these questions so gazing at your companion and knowing their own difficulty will be simple for you.

3. Never impose your own ideas and beliefs.

No matter how much you think in terms of knowledge, wisdom, or even intelligence, you are stronger than your mate, never enforce your own ideas and beliefs. Doing this makes you only ignorant and unsure of how they actually feel.

If you wish to be a spouse with understanding in a partnership, you will know that it is important to respect the values of your spouse and recognize their own views as part of who they are if you want to deepen the connection.

4. Let your partner to live a life outside of your relationship.

Having a spouse with understanding implies knowing that your relationship is not the center of the universe – so the same goes for your significant other. In other terms, don't push your spouse to sacrifice your friendship – and that means allowing them the right to live and have fun, especially if you're not around.

5. Respect your partner's needs as a human being.

Let your companion go out with friends, or share some time with relatives. Let them travel alone, and even in your absence, live their lives to the fullest. Above everything, let them follow their specific goal and inspire them to step out into the world to fulfill their biggest dreams.

6. Remember that you are not always right.

Having an understanding companion in terms of the preceding segment implies listening to what the other individual has to say. You aren't always correct, so much of the time, attempting to show that your opinions, thoughts, and decision are more reasonable will upset your spouse more and could even contribute to a dispute rather than a resolution.

7. Learn how to compromise.

If you wish to be an understanding partner, you have to focus on finding common ground, choosing to agree to disagree, rather than repeatedly pointing out that you're always right. Note, your spouse isn't the opponent, so you both fight the same war.

8. Give your partner opportunity to explain before reacting.

When you believe your partner has done anything to make you feel frustrated, irritated, or sad, give them an opportunity to justify. Hear the tale from their perspective, and don't be swift with your judgment. People in a partnership often seem to prefer rage and respond to destructive emotional outbursts before they really speak with their spouse.

9. Understand your partner's intentions and motivations.

That the most difficult thing to do is to know how to think, particularly when your partner has done something wrong, especially if you feel upset and cheated, you ought to find the courage and the affection to care, though, with utter honesty. More significantly, you must maintain trust in your partner, and allow them the ability to clarify their motivations and what inspired them to do so.

10. Always choose kindness over anger.

In connection with the previous sections, if there are instances where you find your partner to be at fault, you always have to choose to be kind rather than to allow anger to make things worse. Anger will never solve anything, especially if you have done something that could potentially end your relationship with your significant other.

Anger can be a normal response to an event or an action that hurts you, but especially if you want to fix a dying relationship, it is the wrong direction. Being more compassionate involves opting to be caring and gentle, helping you to grow together when attempting to make things work.

11. Help your partner learn from their mistakes.

Another means of fixing an already ruined friendship is to be understanding. It will allow you to recover and realize that even though your partner made mistakes, they also deserve the second opportunity to prove himself/herself again.

You have to play your role in the relationship in this phase by letting them understand significant other lessons about their faults. You have to remain careful and have the knowledge to give things another try. More significantly, try to concentrate on the initiative instead of the faults they made.

12. Encourage your partner to be more open.

Not everybody understands how to convey their thoughts and emotions into words, and even in an intimate relationship, that fact is a challenge. First of all, if they don't really know how to articulate their emotions and communicate their innermost feelings, how can you understand someone? You have got to be more careful with this case.

Encourage your companion to be more transparent regarding issues that may impact your partnership explicitly or indirectly. You would then have the correct and transparent degree of understanding as to how you will manage any unforeseen challenges you encounter as a couple every day.

3.3 Understanding leading towards the Healthy Relationship?

Every relation is special, and there are several different explanations why people come together. Part of what determines a good partnership is having a shared vision about both what you aspire to be and where you expect the relationship to go. And that's something you'll only learn if you speak to your partner sincerely and frankly. There are also some characteristics that most stable marriages have in general, however. Knowing these fundamental values will help sustain positive, satisfying, and thrilling relationships whatever ambitions you strive for or obstacles you encounter together.

Try to maintain a meaningful emotional connection with each other.

You make one feel happy and emotionally fulfilled with each other. There is a distinction between being loved and feeling loved. It makes you feel valued and appreciated by your spouse when you feel loved because someone really does understand you. Some couples are trapped in happy coexistence even without the couples becoming really emotionally connected to each other. While on the surface, the relationship may appear successful, a lack of continuing interaction and personal link just brings distance between two individuals.

You're not afraid of (respectful) disagreement.

Some people calmly work it out while others can lift their voices and argue strongly. However, the trick in a good connection is not to be afraid of confrontation. You must feel free to mention issues that concern you without fear of retaliation, and you must be able to settle disputes without embarrassment, disrespect, or fixation on being right.

You keep outside relationships and interests alive.

Given the promises of romantic novels or films, nobody can fulfill all the needs. In reality, it will place undue stress on a partnership to demand so much from your spouse. It is necessary to retain your own identity outside of the relationship to promote and enhance your intimate relationship, sustain relationships with family and friends, and retain your hobbies and interests.

You communicate openly and honestly.

Effective communication is an integral part of every relationship. It will improve trust and reinforce the connection between you as both partners realize what they expect from the partnership and are confident sharing their needs, concerns, and desires.

3.4 Falling in Love vs. Staying in Love

Normally, falling in love just appears to happen for certain people. It is remaining in love — or maintaining the feeling of "falling in love "— that involves effort and dedication. But, with its benefits, the commitment is well worth it. A happy, stable romantic relationship will act as an enduring pillar of support and joy in your life, improving all facets of your wellbeing through good and bad times. You will create a lasting relationship that lasts — even for a lifetime — by taking measures now to maintain or rekindle the falling in love experience.

Many partners often concentrate on their relationships while there are real, unavoidable obstacles to resolve.

When the issues are settled, they frequently shift their focus back to their jobs, babies, or other desires. Romantic partnerships, therefore, involve constant dedication and devotion to a fruitful marriage. This would take your commitment and energy as long as the wellbeing of an intimate partnership is essential to you. And now, finding and resolving the minor issues in your partnership will also help keep it from becoming worse down the track. The following advice will help maintain the feeling of falling in love and keep the romantic partnership healthy.

Tip 1: Spend some quality time face to face

Looking and speaking to one another, you fall in love. When you carry on looking and listening in the same diligent ways, you will sustain the long-term falling in love experience. You still have some nice thoughts of the first time you met your loved one. Everything seemed fresh and exciting, so you often spent hours either talking or coming up with cool new ideas to try. However, as time goes by, the pressures of jobs, families, other responsibilities, and the desire for the time we all have for ourselves will make it more challenging to spend time together.

Many people notice that they are slowly replacing the face-to-face interaction of their early dating days with rushed calls, emails, and instant messaging. Although digital contact is perfect for many reasons, it does not impact the brain and nervous system positively in the same way as face-to-face communication. It's nice to give your companion a text or voice message saying, "I love you," but if you never look at them or take the opportunity to sit down together, they'll always believe you don't understand or respect them. And, as a couple, you may become more distant or isolated. The emotional signals that both of you need to feel appreciated can only be conveyed in person, and no matter how busy life is, it is necessary to spend time together.

Enact to spend some quality time together on a daily basis.

No matter how occupied you are, take a couple of minutes per day to put your electronic devices down, quit worrying about other stuff, and just concentrate on and communicate with your spouse.

Find something that you enjoy doing together.

Try something fun, whether it's a common hobby, a dance class, a quick stroll, or sitting over a morning cup of coffee.

Try something new together.

A fun way to reconnect and keep things interesting can be to do new things together. It can be as easy as trying out a new restaurant or going on a day trip to a place you have never been to before.

Focus on having fun together.

During the early phases of a relationship, couples are sometimes more humorous and fun. Often, however, this positive mind-set may be lost when life problems tend to get in the way or old resentments continue to mount up. In fact, maintaining a sense of humor can help you get through tough times, reduce stress, and work through issues more easily. Think of affectionate ways to surprise your partner, such as bringing flowers home or booking a table in their favorite restaurant in an unexpected way. Playing with dogs or little ones will help you reconnect with your fun side too.

Do things together that benefit others.

One of the most significant ways to remain near and linked is to concentrate together on something outside of the relationship that you and your spouse enjoy. Volunteering for a campaign, initiative, or community service that each of you has value will keep a relationship new and exciting. It can also introduce you both to new experiences and perspectives, give you the ability to solve new problems together and have fresh opportunities to connect.

As well as helping to alleviate agony, anxiety, and depression, there is great satisfaction in doing something for others to gain. Humans are hard-wired for supporting others—the further that you support, the better that you feel — as individuals and as a couple.

Tip 2: Stay connected through communication

Effective communication is a key part of a successful relationship. You'll feel comfortable and secure when you have a healthy interpersonal bond with your spouse. When people stop interacting well, they stop connected well, and periods of transition or uncertainty will really bring the separation out. It may sound complicated, but you will generally navigate through the challenges you have as long as you communicate.

Tell your partner what you want clearly. Don't make them guess.

Conversing about what you need isn't always convenient. For one, several of us, in a relationship, do not invest enough time talking about what is really important to us. So even though you realize what you need, it may make you feel insecure, humiliated, or even shy of thinking about it. Yet look at things from the point of view of your partner. It's a pleasure to give warmth and empathy to those you love, not a burden.

When you have known each other for some time, you may believe your companion has a fairly clear sense of what you're thinking and what you need. Your partner isn't a mind-reader, though. While your spouse may have an idea, voicing your desires clearly is far better to prevent misunderstanding. Your companion might feel something, but maybe this isn't what you need. What's more, people are adapting, and for example, what you needed and desired five years ago can be quite different now. So instead of allowing frustration, confusion, or rage to develop as your spouse gets it wrong all the time, get used to telling them precisely what you need.

Take note of your partner's nonverbal cues.

Too much of our communication is expressed by what we don't tell. Nonverbal signals, which involve eye contact, voice tone, stance, and movements like leaning down, crossing your arms, or holding someone's hand, convey far better than words. If you are able to pick up nonverbal signals or "body language" from your partner, you would be able to tell them how they really feel and react accordingly. Every individual needs to recognize their own, and the nonverbal signals of their spouse, for a relationship to develop well. Reactions from your partner may be different from yours. For starters, one person may need a romantic form of conversation after a frustrating day — whereas another may only want to go for a stroll or relax and talk together.

It's always important to make sure that your body language matches what you mean. If you claim "I am fine," but you clench your teeth and turn away, then your expression obviously shows that you are anything but "normal." You feel cherished and content when you get encouraging emotional indications from your spouse, and your spouse feels the same when you give positive emotional signals. When you avoid having an interest in the feelings of your own or your spouse, you will deteriorate the bond between you and your ability to interact may suffer, particularly in periods of stress.

Be a good listener

Although much focus is put on communicating in our society, if you can learn to communicate in a way that helps another person feel respected and heard, you can create a deeper, stronger bond between you. There is a significant difference between listening and actually understanding in this manner. If you actively listen — while you're concerned in what's being discussed — you're able to notice the slight intonations in the voice of your companion, showing you how they actually sound and the feelings they're

119

attempting to convey. Being a great listener is not about agreeing with your partner or changing your mind. But it can help you identify specific viewpoints that will help you overcome disputes.

Manage stress

You are more prone to misread your intimate partner while you are anxious or mentally exhausted, give contradictory or off-putting nonverbal messages, or lapse into inappropriate knee-jerk behavior trends. How often do you feel overwhelmed and fly off your loved one's handle and say or do something that you eventually regretted? When you will learn to handle stress easily and return to a calm environment, not only can you prevent these regrets, but you can even help reduce conflicts and misunderstandings — and also help relax your companion as tempers build up.

Tip 3: Keep physical intimacy alive

Touch is a core part of human existence. Infant studies also have shown the significance of daily, affective communication for brain growth. And the advantages don't end in childhood. Affectionate contact boosts the levels of oxytocin in the body, a hormone influencing bonding and attachment.

Although sex is always a cornerstone of a stable relationship, the only form of sexual contact may not be that. Equally significant is the frequent, affectionate touch — holding hands, hugging, kissing.

Of course, being mindful of what your partner likes is vital. Unwanted touching or inappropriate overtures can tense and retreat the other person – exactly what you don't want. Like in so many other facets of a healthy relationship, that can be due to how much you interact with your mate over your desires and thoughts.

And if you have to worry about stressful workloads or young kids, you can help maintain physical intimacy alive by sneaking out some regular couple time, whether it's in the context of a date night or even an hour at the end of the day where you can relax and chat or hold hands.

Tip 4: Learn to balance the give and take ratio in your relationship

If you're expecting to get what you want in a relationship 100 percent of the time, you're setting up for frustration. Compromise creates strong relationships. However, ensuring that there is a fair exchange of effort required on the part of each person.

Recognize what's important to your partner

Knowing what truly means to your mate will go a long way in fostering mutual goodwill and a consensus setting. On the flip side, it's always critical that your spouse understands your desires and that you explicitly state them. Spending endlessly on others at the detriment of your own desires can only create frustration and rage.

Don't make "winning" your goal

It would be difficult to reach a solution if you tackle your partner with the mentality that things ought to be your way, or else. This mentality often stems from not getting the needs fulfilled when being younger, or it may be years of cumulative frustration in the relationship hitting a boiling point. Getting firm opinions on things is fine, but your spouse always needs to be understood. Be mindful of the other individual, and of their perspective.

Learn how to respectfully resolve conflict

Conflict is unavoidable in every relationship, so both partners need to believe they've been understood to maintain a strong relationship. The ultimate goal is not to win but to preserve and strengthen the relationship.

Make sure you are fighting fair.

Keep your focus on the issue and value the other person. Don't begin disputes over issues that are unchangeable.

Don't attack someone directly.

But use the "I" statements to express how you felt. For e.g., try "I feel bad when you do that" instead of saying, "You make me feel bad."

Don't drag old arguments into the mix.

Rather of digging into previous disputes or grudges, and assigning blame, concentrate on what you might do to fix the issue in the here and now.

Be willing to forgive.

By being unwilling or unable to forgive anyone, dispute settlement is impossible.

If tempers flare, take a break.

Take a few minutes to relieve the tension and cool yourself before you say anything or do something that you would regret. Mind that you are arguing with the one you love.

Know when to let something go.

If an agreement cannot be made, agree to disagree. It needs two individuals to go on with the argument. If there is a disagreement, you may opt to disengage and move on.

Tip 5: Be ready for ups and downs

It's important to remember that any relationship has ups and downs. You're not always going to be on the same page. One partner can also deal with the problem that affects them, such as the loss of a dear family member. Other incidents, such as job loss or serious health conditions, may impact both spouses and find it impossible to interrelate. You may have various thoughts regarding handling budgets or raising kids. Different individuals cope differently with stress, and misunderstandings may easily turn to irritation and frustration.

Don't vent out your problems with your partner.

The stresses of life will keep us agitated. If you're feeling a lot of stress, it might seem better to vent with your companion and feel much safer to snap at them. Initially, fighting like this may sound like a relief, but it destroys the relationship gradually. Find other strategies to control the anxiety, rage, and frustration more healthily.

Trying to forcefully implement a solution can cause even more problems.

Everyone is struggling on their own journey through challenges and issues. Remember, you are a unit. Continuing together to move on, will bring you past the rough patches.

Look back to the early stages of your relationship.

Share the memories that put the two of you together, discuss the stage at which you started to drift apart, and determine whether you might work together to rekindle the feeling of being in love.

Be open to change.

Change is necessary in life, and whether you go for it, or fight it, it will happen. Flexibility is important to respond to the transition that often takes place in every relationship, and it helps you to evolve together in both the positive and the rough times.

If you need outside help for your relationship, reach out together.

Things in a partnership may often feel too difficult or daunting to manage as a couple. Couples may improve by counseling or communicating with a close relative or religious leader.

Should you be the More Understanding One in the Relationship?

Most people have this "no more Mr. Nice Guy" mentality towards relationships that may be harmful in practical terms. In a relationship, you want a woman to respect you, but at the same time, you need to accept her for it to truly succeed. But, in your relationship, would you be the more understanding?

Essentially, we find the question's assumption to be false. It's not that someone in a relationship should or should not be more or less patient than someone else. It's that anyone of you has to do your best and learn the way you articulate yourself. And how do you connect more and make your relationships happy and more successful in that way?

Active Listening

This one is big. Just like you, the woman needs to be understood in your relationship. She deserves to hear well then that she is being heard. Effective communication is the primary approach to achieve this. How do you do that?

It starts by actually listening to her, and not only waiting for your turn to talk. Then you want to sort of repeat what she said — the emotional essence of it, what she was getting into when she talked. You do so to let her know you've been listening but just to make sure you've understood what she said before you react. Responding to what she has not really mentioned will make her sound confused and make things go south very quickly.

Only after both of these things have been completed, it is time to react.

Owning Your Feelings

It's good to talk about yourself rather than just about anyone else "made" you feel. Owning your thoughts — even possession over all your actions — is a healthy practice to develop. Within a relationship, it has advantages well beyond comprehension or perhaps improved communication. Never place how she made you feel on her, no matter how deeply you thought it was her who made you feel like that. Just talk about how stuff makes you look, instead.

Remember

This can be very hard to recall, particularly when it's the head of the moment. But remember, you must unless you want to keep having the same kinds of arguments over and over and over again. Often it will help you make notes of certain stuff, or just provide one-word reminders about things you want to recall when stuff gets heated up.

3.5 Be Understanding — Whatever That Means For You as a Man

For being the most emotionally sensitive, men in relationships are not understanding. That's not, though, a "yes or no" statement. Apparently, it's a scale. Through the relationships, you should continually strive for greater understanding, so that it can go smoothly in the future. Do not feel like constructing Rome in one day. Look to changing and improving yourself continuously.

After all, that's what life is about really — keeping stuff going along always. It is the core of male selfimprovement, and you should use it in the same manner as every other part of your life in a relationship.

Regardless of how perceptive someone is, knowing other people's feelings isn't always easy, particularly in relationships. There are so many explanations of why your partner may feel like he never emotionally knows you. You may not interact well, you may unintentionally be passive hostile, or you may be way too quick to get mad. This may even have anything to do with your partner because they might not be in tune with their emotions and so cannot perceive theirs. Whatever the case might be, feeling misunderstood, particularly in regard to a relationship, is never pleasant.

So before we venture into all the directions to understand each other more, take a second, and focus on your go-to conversation method. "We get emotionally shocked a number of times in relationships, and we just respond, rather than having the time to label how we actually feel and be honest on what we need," dating Coach Corinne Dobbas, says. "We get angry, and we don't realize why we're so mad, so we always want our partner to recognize why we're angry and understand us." Since no one's a mind reader, it's clear that this solution might not help. Slowing down, picking the words, and giving attention to how you are viewed will be a great approach to manage a heated moment. "In other terms, you will really have a constructive dialogue where the aim is to learn each other, rather than being aggressive, frustrated, or crazy," says Dobbas. Here are a couple of other strategies to keep calm, channel your feelings, connect efficiently and, as a result, ideally "get" one another.

1. Use as Many "I" Statements as Possible

Rule number one: wherever possible, avoid "you" phrases. "People like to argue with expressions like 'you still...' or 'you never...' which might feel like an allegation, 'It's more productive to say 'I feel upset when you...' instead.' This way, the discussion is about how you feel, rather than what your companion might or might not be doing wrong.

2. Keep It Short And Sweet

While you might be eager to spill all of your concerns in one session, doing so might be completely daunting to your companion and perhaps detrimental. If you have something sensitive to tell, it is best to keep it brief and simple. Otherwise, your companion may get confused with their feelings and tuning it out.

3. Focus on Understanding Them

If your companion still feels confused, stepping out of their own head and into yours would be hard for them. So make sure you consider them — what does annoy them, their point of view, etc. — before you attempt to argue on a point. Emotional interaction is a two-way path. Until you attempt to emotionally understand your spouse, it would be impossible for your spouse to try and understand you.

4.   Keep Your Voice Calm

If you're always raising your voice, remaining quiet and knowing each other would really be difficult. So be vigilant with your pace and your tone. "Keeping your voice soft and polite." If it rises, it'll be more challenging for your partner to understand or relate to you.

5.   Pay Attention to Your Body Language

Body language is another aspect that will influence the response of your companion to you and therefore making it more complicated for them to actually "get" what you need. For instance, if you're standing with your arms crossed, you'll look closed off — and maybe even a little guarded. Start calming, first. Keep the body as relaxed and comfortable as possible while attempting to convey complicated emotions.

6.   Make Emotions Part of   Your Daily Conversation

When you two aren't in the habit of expressing emotions, a perfect way to initiate is to build an atmosphere where talking about feelings is totally OK. So one way to do this is to ask open-ended questions to them. "So instead of asking things like, 'How was your day?' consider something like, 'what was the best thing about your day, and why?' as it encourages your partner to express more. That can help expressing feelings sound natural, and you will have more productive discussions going forward.

7.   Be Clearer About How You Feel

Try to be straightforward and to-the-point rather than being passive hostile, or hinting about what you need and hoping your partner would pick on. You might suggest something straightforward like, "If you glance at your screen all the time, I feel like I'm not important to you. Without your cell, I'd just spend more time being with you. Would you want to be less on your screen while we're together?" It covers four things: what's troubling you, how you feel about it, what'd make you feel better, and whether or not you'd feel better. "And though the proposal is not feasible for your partner, you are going to require consideration of the topic at hand. **8. Don't Criticize or Ask Them to Change**

Resist the temptation to clutter your discussion with complaints or suggestions for improvement, and keep it all about your emotions instead. It's crucial to concentrate on expressing your own perspective while thinking about emotions, because you're either searching for, learning, or understanding — not something else. Whether there is a suggestion for improvement or criticism connected to expressing your own feelings, personal awareness would be distracting.

9. **Tell Them They Don't Need To "Fix" Anything**

   It is totally natural for partners to switch into "fix it mode because it is painful to see someone we care about so distressed. So that will place a lot of pressure on the other significant person (even though it is self-imposed strain), and it can make you feel like they aren't listening.

That's why you would want to try to reassure your mate that they don't have to give any suggestions right from the beginning. Tell the person they should not want to make you feel better, but only want them to acknowledge how you feel.

10. Be Smart Regarding when you Decide To Open Up

Choose the time carefully because you decide to get a heart-to-heart, and always sound comprehensible. "It's not a perfect moment to speak up while the significant partner is half asleep, struggling to reach a job deadline, battling traffic, or enjoying a movie or television show they're focusing on. Chats during car rides may be perfect as they don't involve scheduled discussions or frequent eye contact, any of which may render an individual anxious.

11. Figure out How to Speak Their "Language"

Not everyone communicates the same way, and you're going to want to find out how your partner communicates, and whilst still making them understand how you communicate. There is a clear difference between the inability to learn and lack of attention or care.

12. Try to Connect When only you're Not Feeling Emotional

When you feel misunderstood, the middle of a heated debate isn't the time to put things that way. Ironically, the only way to get your mate to personally respond to you is to restrict how intensely you are feeling right now. Sometimes a significant other may go through their own fight-or-flight mode when confronted with a highly emotional spouse, particularly if they believe the relationship is in danger. When you're still in the intensely charged state, so little gets heard or conveyed.

13. Do not feel afraid To Take Some Time Out for your partner

When things get tense, and you don't feel listened to, don't be scared to stop on the discussion and reconvene later on. "Notice what's going on within your body is your heart pounding too fast? Does your skin feel hot? Are you running through the same words in your mind? Take a break, walk away, concentrate on something new for a couple of minutes, and relax back into your body.

14. Say It in Letter Form

When you feel like you're not willing to bring your feeling into sentences, why not pursue a different format? Start writing as a means of describing your partner's emotionally intense issues in a way you can articulate them accurately. It will allow you some time to think about what you'd like to tell and offer your companion time to read and respond.

15. Maintain Reasonable Expectations

Bear in mind; if you two are not on the same page right now, it's totally OK. "People have varying personal backgrounds, and not everyone resonates with everyone." A partner may not really appreciate or understand the experience you have. If your companion isn't very comfortable with their own personal background, it's much more doubtful they won't 'notice' yours. Think of emotional understanding as a target to aspire for. "Just keep communicating, no matter what. That's the secret to truly knowing each other and to more effectively share the feelings.

Chapter 04: Self-Evaluation

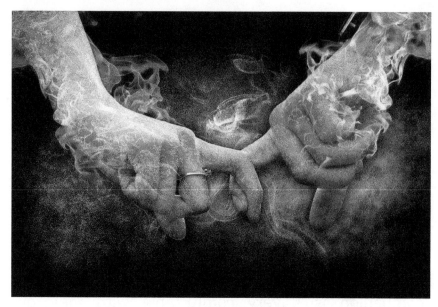

How to evaluate yourself in a relationship and the methods to do so are discussed in this chapter.

Questions for the evaluation and dimensions upon which one should try to improve are also discussed.

4.1 Would You Date Yourself?

Here's why self-assessment is essential for healthy relationships

If you could date yourself, do you think you'd be satisfied and pleased with the marriage or the relationship?

When you're single and ready for a relationship, but nothing appears to fall out, there's a temptation to find yourself, see your fantastic attributes and pretty features, and believe that you're good and it's only for a right moment when someone amazing comes along.

Yet, then, is it going to be a question of time, or of change?

Perhaps the singularity is not so much a perception problem as it is a self-delusion concern. What if you're not always as smart as you let yourself believe? What if you're just doing great but always fall shy of the criteria required to attract the kind of man or woman you've seen in your mind?

You know, it's easy to conjure in your head the vision of a perfect partner, but it's not that straightforward to have an acceptable visual image of yourself. This would not be that easy to agree perhaps. You may also not be as cool as you believe you are.

If and that's why it's necessary to ask yourself the introspective question honestly-' would I date myself? 'And still, create painfully frank selfassessments if you do so. That should, by the way, be very regular.

That could be where the secret for you to find a partner lies. There is a persistent need for selfassessment, particularly among people who are currently dating and others who are still married, to continuously see one's self through the simple lens of candid introspection.

You will be realistic and selfless enough to question yourself; if he or she behaves this way, would I be satisfied with my partner? Should I feel happy with them handling me like this? Would I really blame them for this kind of behavior?

Whether there are any moral defects in you that anyone else will never tolerate, don't be selfishly deluded into believing they'd take that from you.

This is not the way it functions. When you wouldn't want it, bring yourself to work on it and genuinely aspire to grow more. Not only has your [potential] partner needed this!

Repeatedly, by doing so, you are becoming a stronger version of yourself up to the point that you become comfortable enough to respond in the affirmative when you are asked: "Should you date yourself? "It's not that convenient to be selfanalytical as it appears. That's why the selfassessment report you've got to do at work is already sitting on your desk waiting to conclude.

So that sort of self-analysis is important while you are in a relationship. What can you do to boost your relation? What do you need to bring in there from your husband or wife?

If you're prepared to go deep into your own brain to improve your relationship's wellbeing, here's where to start:

(1) Learn How to Pick Up On Your Own Patterns

If you want to make a difference in your to-do list in your everyday life, serious consideration will slip to the bottom of your priorities. This is why it's necessary to set aside time and take a look back to see if your actions relate to your relationship (both positive and negative). Journaling is a perfect opportunity to get a snapshot of the acts you perform and the thoughts you keep on revisiting. **(2) Don't Be Afraid To Over-Communicate**

You don't want to undermine the intellect of your spouse, and you believe that out of your relationship, they realize what you expect and need. Yet you know what they're doing about presuming — it's real. And if it seems your desires are clear, don't be shy to ask your boyfriend or girlfriend to be precise. Let them know just how they can make you feel relaxed and comfortable.

(3) Be Generous With Your Praise

When your significant other is doing anything less than perfect, it's easy to get cynical, so if you're going to judge, you ought to be able to make constructive feedback. Consider the effect "yelp." Most people just dream about writing a comment when they've had a terrible restaurant encounter, so when it's all peachy, they just go ahead with their day. Make it a point to praise your boo as well as you condemn it in a positive way. You are loving how they made dinner while you were having an especially stressful day? Admire the expertise in preparing their trip? Let's just let them know.

(4) Don't Immediately Reject Criticism

Hearing criticism may be difficult, particularly when it comes from someone you love, but this support is important if the relationship is to be further strengthened. When your companion gives you thoughts on what they need, be open to the input, and ready to adapt when necessary.

(5) Don't Let Outside Stresses Put Extra Pressure on Your Relationship

A celebration is coming up. If this individual is "The One" or if / when you get married, you feel this constant stress. All of a sudden ordinary talk appears to get even more complex, and in all, you are trying to seek a secret context. It will draw on a close relation and make it uncomfortable. When you're an adult, outdoor tension comes with the territory so make it a point to accept your relationship for what it is. Don't allow relatives, friends, or other influences to put pressure on you and trigger stress and spill through your relationship.

4.2 Self-Evaluation & Preparation for Relationship Success

Self-evaluation can be difficult, but the benefits can be fantastic. When a self-assessment is done, and the results present the probability of you gaining a relationship of greater quality than you have in the past significantly increases.

Preparation for Success

Preparedness to be in a relationship is essential for its survival. When you're not ready, you're likely to mess things up or indulge in a poor relationship. Even worst, as they step into your world, you won't know the one who is right. An accurate selfassessment will disclose any shortfalls.

-Preparation will continue with a self-assessment. Have you evolved into the type of person in your heart you know you should be? Is your life on track? Is it in equilibrium? An individual starting the path cannot be in a state of need or loss for his ideal lifepartner. They'll need to be secure and stable. Otherwise, they'll be in a relationship that represents their inappropriate state of life.

This self-evaluation includes looking at the four main fields where relationships appear to have the most influence: emotional, physical, social, and financial.

Emotional

Have you achieved emotional maturity, or are you already holding lingering trauma from a previous hurtful relationship or a traumatic childhood? If so, first get it settled! Speak to a buddy, read any books about self-help, or visit a therapist or clergy.

Have you mastered your subconscious by taking care of your thought content? Have you learned of your emotions' incredible strength and how they decide your attitude, physiology, and fate? If not, purchase some books, tapes, or attend a lecture on the matter. Then use the knowledge to build your intellectual strength to use your emotions to function for you instead. It is important to become an expert in this field, as it will influence almost every aspect of your life, including your capability to find a spouse who is right for you.

Have you made up a list of core beliefs and short- and long-term goals? If not, then do now! Write down the principles and the goals. Give it a path to your future. Create a roadmap for life you dream of, and the person you desire to be along the way.

Physical

Are you happy with your appearance, dietary habits, and training program? It doesn't mean that when you continue your journey, you need to be at your perfect weight, fitness routine, or food schedule. But this does suggest you need a full embrace and respect for your body.

If not, take steps immediately to reduce weight, begin a regimen of exercise, and set up a diet plan. Only taking the pledge and being frank will be what it takes for you to achieve self-acceptance.

Yet don't deceive yourself, because the mental boost of making the first major move in completing a weight-reduction plan, purchasing a gym card or signing up for a fitness course would just be fleeting. You have to carry the job through and stick with it. It takes about six weeks to develop a new habit, experts claim. This period of time will be a fair beginning of stamina, contributing to the outcomes you expect.

Social

It's necessary to have social equilibrium in a relationship. Finally, exclusive dependence on a mate for all of your social nourishment and comfort will place so much burden on a relationship. It can also significantly limit its potential to satisfy.

Even social interactions that exist outside a relationship may achieve some elements of personal fulfillment. Participation in social events that meet mutual desires, such as belonging to a common community group, will provide the social stimulation needed by each partner. And, unless social conditions are fulfilled, the partnership as a couple becomes significantly beneficial if they're not, so it becomes a misery.

Friendships of your own sex people are often essential to a relationship's progress. There are certain things that only someone of their own gender will grasp. It is not fair to close yourself off from the rest of the world and to ask your companion to accept all the problems that come with being a male or a female. Relying solely on them for advice on these things won't satisfy all of your needs. And the outcome when they are unable to satisfy them is disappointment, aggravation, and turmoil.

The relation a person has with their (same-sex) mates is not a substitution for the intimate bond you share as a couple. It just strengthens it, and even to a significant degree, it does so! Men are consolidating

148

themselves as men through interacting around other guys. Women continue improving themselves as women by bonding with other females. Then, there are romantic sparks as two spiritually replenished couple sync.

Financial

No other single problem tends to break more relationships than financial matters. It's disrespectful to your partner and yourself to get into a relationship without your finances being in order. Just as in all the other aspects we mentioned above, it is important that you both be safe in this field so that your relationship is based on a solid basis, not on the sand and definitely not on quicksand.

Are the accounts in balance then? Would you have the power of your payment cards and other payment producing areas? How is your tax and savings planning? Should you take full advantage of occupational retirement insurance programs? Would you set up a personal investment program? If not, then have it done this instance! Of all, if you want to get them, do you not want to be a provider to the future of you and your partner and that of your children? Clearly, your employment standing plays a key role in your financial wellbeing.

Will you have a successful career? It doesn't say you have to be at your ideal workplace, but then you have to be happy in your current position or move for your target in another way. So you're taking classes at a nearby college or trade school, for example, or you're interested in a promotion for your own new job or company.

4.3 Questions for Self-Evaluation

Use the following questions to gain more clarity.

1. What do we have in common?

It doesn't come as a shock who are alike pull in to the alike. To put it another way, the conventional theory "attracting opposites" is appallingly false.

You may feel drawn to a person that has attributes you don't possess, but in the long run, you're unlikely to be content with them. The variations tend to trigger problems when the attraction and infatuation hormones wear off, and gradually tear you apart.

A group of Beijing researchers reported that people tend to collaborate with someone who has a common lifetime focus. Ru-de Liu, Ran Bian, and colleagues measured the primary motivation of individuals (to meet targets or escape problems), which they described as advancement or protection. They noticed subjects with the same motivation automatically gravitated to men or women.

2. Do we have a strong physical connection?

Mutual physical affection in couples contributes to further intimacy and love-making, which has been shown to help partners connect and sustain contentment in dedicated relationships.

Meltzer, Makhanova, and colleagues observed that an enjoyable session with a partner helped the pair feel better and increased the marital satisfaction rates up to 48 hours. Overall, partners who make love feel great about the spouse and the relationship most frequently.

Within the couple, the absence of intense sexual desire, vice versa, is linked to a poorer relationship.

3. How are we treating ourselves and one another?

- Do you appreciate how one handles you?
- What applies to the way you treat yourself in this relationship?

- Do you appreciate the way you handle your companion or yourself?

- Do you feel satisfied with how you handle your darling?

A stable partnership is the one where all these four questions earn a constructive answer. Every couple can have their own ways to arrange themselves and act in a pair, but when all of you are good about it, problems may continue to pop up constantly.

Individuals are mean with each other in certain couples, or one person uses the second person to vent out grievances. Yet they keep thinking, "We really love one another," Loving isn't a real excuse to behave terribly. The problem needs to be addressed.

4. You, Me, and Us: Is there a stability?

Each relationship has 3 parties: You, your spouse, and the Collective ("Us"). Each of these three entities ought to satisfy the needs. If one person thinks it's all about the partner, then it's a bell of warning. It can be the reverse at times: it's all about "Us" and little consideration of the needs and wishes of each person. It's much more of a concern if there's a sensation that there's no "us".

5. Do we contribute equally?

It's definitely not about making a financial contribution, but putting ongoing and substantial effort into the relationship, which the other person regards as valuable. Often all participants feel as if they are performing all the effort, which suggests they don't consider the second participant's contribution as valuable.

6. Is the relationship reciprocal?

One trend which has been clear over the years, if one person does not want to be in the relationship any longer, it won't survive. Whoever wishes to get out would still consider a problem in what the partner does. Often situations may be restored and patched together if it doesn't fit, but both sides have to show a sincere interest and motivation.

An expert marriage counselor says he essentially knows whether or not a couple has the potential to work things out within the first 5 minutes they come in the session. If the partners sit down on a sofa next to each other, they're offered a chance. Even if they try their utmost to stay as far apart as possible from each other, that's a normal fight failed.

7. Do we have common values?

It is impossible to push forward as a unified front until the fundamental principles are compatible. Your values and ideals will continuously collide. For example, if the most important value of one couple is family, but its liberation for the partner, the couple would suffer.

8. Do we have common goals?

People sometimes initiate a relationship solely based on physical affection, and then discover that they want opposite things in life. For example, Russian women online dating people typically want to get married and have babies, but their partners just want something simple with little commitment. These competing objectives are likely to collide, even though shared desire and attraction are present. Many couples begin their lives together desiring the same things, but through the years, their goals shift. Realigning goals and expectations is an important aspect of holding the partnership intact.

9. Am I a nice person next to my sweetheart?

Some people are putting the best in us, while some are making the exact opposite impact. When you love this person but don't like who you are in their company, this relationship doesn't do any of you any good. Having a self-destructive spouse has a detrimental impact on one's sense of self-worth.

10. If I were to go for a partner today, would I pick the same person?

It is perhaps the most critical query you need to tackle, offering you a clear idea about whether you can stay or leave. If this query is asked, too many people unwaveringly exclaim, "Gosh, NO!" But they still question if it's worth keeping this relationship.

4.4 Dimensions to Self-Evaluate

In reality, that is the problem that we will all continue to pose each day. Evaluation of partnerships is part of upkeep; if one day you are unexpectedly unaware of the solution, it won't take that much focus. Hopefully, then we won't have too many people to leave a terrible partnership, who were 3–10 years late.

Regardless of how long-married couples have been together, they will still learn from talking about how they feel about each other and their relationship at the moment. Putting time aside for routine check-in will help avoid future complications and establish constructive solutions.

A married couple has several approaches to determine how they are progressing, but there are seven dimensions of an interpersonal relationship that are both easy to understand and use as a starting point. These are not meant to cover aspects that might be more special to a specific relationship but may act as a promising start to the queries.

The seven dimensions are presented below.

Dimension Number One — Playing Together

There is no easier way to assess a relationship than to question the spouses when they remember to laugh hard together. Humour and playfulness are part of a good relationship, and at the beginning of many, they are abundant. If playtime is unintentional or scheduled, whether it's regenerating, light-hearted and enjoyable, it's great.

Playtime ensures when you can do anything that you want to do to each other at times when both of you want to. This therefore allows you not to bring previous or potential issues, and put down your burdensome obligations. They become more lighthearted, and happier as couples and perform well together. It's the way people become beautiful children in those instances where time doesn't exist about each other.

1. How much do you still share the same interaction with your partner?

2. How often are you doing something impulsive and funny for your partner?

3. Do you put your stresses behind while you play together with your partner?

4. Will you have each other laughing hard?

5. Do you consider yourself amused in the same situations?

Dimension Number Two — Sharing Dreams

You and your partner should be allowed to express what you feel about issues you know are not part of your everyday lives in a relationship. It can be as easy as thinking about films and books and seeing oneself in those roles. Or, if good luck suddenly fell upon you, you can dream about what you might do.

More practical values are ways you will discuss future goals together, such as where you could travel to or maybe where you would settle when you're older. Exploring those possibilities will lead you to more exciting potential experiences, like dreaming about things you want to improve for yourself or something you'd want to know more. And if they might appear out of the reach of existing possibility, these unique mutual reflections will extend the understanding of each other's inner worlds.

New couples often speak of dreams because they have a relationship ahead of them. More stable couples tend to forget to open themselves up to new opportunities.

You do have the optimistic side of memories, so you will use them to build fresh potential visions. Whatever path is followed, the couples feel committed to expressing anything they may think of without fear of invalidation.

1. How often can you share the abstract thoughts and fantasies with your partner?

2. Do you feel your partner would be interested in your dreams?

3. Can you carry on the intellectual and emotional views of each other?

4. Will you encourage yourself to pursue future dreams without turning them off?

5. Feel safe to share something that's on your wish list?

Dimension Number Three — Trust

Hopefully, in your innermost thoughts and emotions, you and your partner trust each other confidently and will talk about almost everything without fear of judgment, humiliation, or contempt. When something is awful, you come to each other first and believe in the ability of your partner to listen and help.

And when things appear normal, you're always going through a constant emotional and mental experience, and you're never shocked by something that you don't anticipate. As fresh ideas or emotions surface, you're always able to invest in the effort it takes and stay up-to-date and seek and learn and transform for each other.

Trust is at the center of a strong romantic partnership. You know your partner has integrity, honesty, and responsibility for what he or she says. You should always depend on the fact that if something shifts with the way he or she thinks about you, your companion can inform you directly.

This dimension is where the most relevant skill is communication. Your aim is to keep from being aggressive, emotional, or offended when the relationship distresses your spouse, and allow them to open up. If kindness and motivation are the first reactions, you'll know more about the hidden problems that might be behind what's being mentioned.

1. Do you share critical thoughts and emotions with your partner without fear of distress?

2. Do you think your spouse listens closely to your concerns when you're worried over something important?

3. Can you count on having your partner here when you need him or her?

4. Do you consider your companion as your best friend?

5. Do you trust your companion to keep your emotions and inner thoughts sacred?

Dimension Number Four — Working together as a Team.

All romantic couples should work together to address the difficulties and problems of life if they intend to remain emotionally connected. Everybody understands they should all be performing their best as members of the team with whatever is being requested. They gladly step over, too, if the other has a valid reason to drop back immediately, knowing that the responsibilities of the relationship would level back with time.

Some couples decide in advance what their individual roles as members of the team will be, while others prefer to exchange many of their roles as they see fit at the time, or do more of them together. In any case, both of you feel confident that you can work out disagreements while keeping in mind your mutual goals. You depend on each other with no fear that either he or she may not do what they have agreed to do.

1. Can you count on your partner to do his or her part when there is a task to be done?

2. Do you think your partner fulfill his or her promises?

3. Can you trust your partner to let you know whether he or she is unable to fulfill their promised commitment?

4. Do you feel at peace as you operate together with the allocation of obligation and effort?

5. If you disagree and come up with alternative ideas, do you talk about things?

Dimension Number Five — Successful Debaters

The romantic relationship rationales generate mutual tension on both spouses. These appear to be tackled even as one person gives up to another, causing frustration and loss. Partners who seek to transform their disputes into optimal strategies expect responses to be discovered that can make them feel as satisfied as possible.

In the same case, when the two of you do not see eye-to-eye, you can always listen closely to each other's point of view. You realize it's important to keep the desires of your companion as close to your heart as you do yours.

Couples who may conflict with each other's consideration, appreciation, and empathy are far more likely to consider alternatives that bring them closer to a new truth. They say it is not. Rather, they master the skill of discussion, realizing they will be prepared to sound and react like their spouses do when they are called upon to do so.

1. When you see yourself in a dispute where you are being an antagonist, both of you decide to stay silent, give it some time, and come back with a more cooperative mind-set.

2. Do you find like resolving disputes equally with your partner?

3. Do you freely appeal to your partner's point of view while you are in a conflict?

4. Do you believe your companion should listen to your desires and accept them when they disagree with his or her own?

5. Do you find both of your expectations in your solutions?

6. If asked, could you exactly represent the position of your partner?

Dimension Number Six — Parenting the Child in your Partner

Not only are we the age we are today, we are all the ages we have ever been. Memories are basically opportunities to travel back in time and remember the way we were then. As a consequence, there are moments that your romantic companion may symbolically regard you as a parent. For several partners, this aspect of a partnership may be the toughest to manage.

Your current encounters with the relationship can cause conscious or unconscious responses from the past experiences you have had. The way we react to the terms, gestures, facial expressions, voice intonations, and touch from the person with whom we share our life in the present is nearly impossible not to have those early memories impact.

Would you want to raise a kid like your real partner? Would you have handled the kid differently despite what you already learn about him or her? What in his or her personality will you admire or despise? How can you help the child feel cherished but still respond in ways you considered advantageous to both of you?

1. Do you think the characteristics of your spouse will be likable to you if he or she were your own child?

2. Will you feel sympathy for his struggles?

3. Would you want to alter his or her behavior?

4. Would he or she sound lucky to have you as a parent?

5. Would you feel confident doing a successful job that will raise him or her?

Dimension Number Seven — Would the Child in You Want Your Partner as a Parent?

This query, seen from the other side of the equation, is the complement to the above. Your spouse will always discipline you symbolically like he or she has been parented like an infant. Looking at the upbringing of your parents, you will see how the method of raising a kid has changed, and how it has influenced the actions of your relationship toward you.

Parental conduct reactions will run the gamut from satisfyingly pleasurable to intensely offensive. With time, those reactions tend to increase. What could have started as tolerant and supportive responses can morph into more critical statements like, "You start drinking too much, just like your father," or "Your mother is incredibly cheap. If you're beginning to feel "parented" in a way that exudes anger, pain, or alienation, you have to tell your spouse how you feel, and why. On the other side, when you are upset or relieving you while you are down, you may love the way your companion cradles you. It is crucial that "parental" behaviors when you were small do not re-wound you the way they did. When partners may recognize them, instead, they will substitute their reactions with ones that can relieve the sorrows of childhood.

1. Does your wife offer support for you in a helpful fashion when you require meaningful parental care?

2. Do you feel your companion will give you that when you feel childlike, insecure, and wanting comfort?

3. Can your partner put away his or her needs when you ask, and be there for you?

4. Can your counterpart discern between symbolically parenting you in a positive way, instead of having you feel worse?

5. Would you have wished that your partner was your parent?

Your answers to these questions may evolve strikingly over time and with each stage of your relationship, but if you regularly check them out, you can see where you have been, where you might be going as a relationship, and any changes you might need to make.

4.4 Evaluating the State of Relationship

Making a decision to marry or to stay together is a major change, rife with naturally its share of uncertainty over what could follow. Below is a collection of questions to ask yourself and ask each other as a partner, a point of starting for a dialogue to recognize your strengths and see where future issues can lay. You should see this as a means of measuring the relationship's current situation, an activity to perform on your own, or preferably, as a couple.

Those are:

1. Do you argue?

- If you do, are you in a position to hold disputes getting out of hand?

- Would you come around to address the issue objectively to come to a solution?

This one has a lot to it. Arguing is somewhat in the beholder's eyes — it may be defined as a foursentence exchange with some snapping and huffing for some couples, while others may include only decibel levels above 60 or the use of curse words. The capacity for either or both of you to brake when you believe the discussion is no longer a discussion but has reached emotionally unsafe terrain is significant.

Keeping the disputes from out of control is about self-regulation and self-consciousness. What's hard when you're upset is to avoid the tunnel vision that makes you want to make your point and fight for it to death. Getting upset is okay, but it is important to realize when the conversation goes nowhere and turns into a struggle for power. If you can, and can stop so it won't escalate further, you've perfected an essential skill in relationships.

On the contrary side of the coin are those couples who go out of their way to completely avoid a confrontation. Both couples are walking on eggshells, feeling risky to share their feelings. Differences are swept under the rug, and distance is used to prevent conflict. Deep love and interaction is impossible when moving intense feelings to the edge, so difficulties are rarely fixed and instead accumulate. The relationship is likely to grow progressively disengaged and shallow over time.

Circling back is the second half of any claim, and where couples will quickly get trapped. Circling back involves going around and fixing the problem, whether it all breaks apart in a tense dispute or has been washed out too easily. What's all-too-easy to do is start and stop with an apology—"Sorry last night "— but don't go back and dig into the argument's actual source. Why? For what? Because you are afraid another argument will start. The paradoxical move is to step up and talk about the issue in order to bring it to rest.

2. How do you make decisions?

It is naturally also linked to the first issue concerning arguments — the method of dilemma solving. Yet choices are mostly about figuring out what sorts of things really ought to be discussed as a person. It goes through the limits and the turf: I don't even worry about decorating the interior, and I don't know what sofa you want. And, I admire your ability to handle income, and I feel confident managing the finances with you. Or, no, my home life is vital to me, and I deserve to have a say on the couch; or, I'm worried about money readily, and we need to sit down together and work out a budget.

It's about material — what sorts of issues we ought to discuss together as a couple, so we settle about what they are — and the method — how we will have rational, constructive discussions. It's also often about learning how you handle each information and make decisions — that Tom, for instance, wants to do a lot of work on major topics and requires time to figure things out; he's not a guy you should force to think on his feet too.

But decision-making often carries with it fundamental power issues: does every spouse communicate their feelings, or does one party appear to take responsibility? Was the decisionmaking process calm and accessible, or full of fear and walking-on-eggshells?

3. Do you know what your partner is most sensitive to?

It is about getting to know the emotional wounds and trigger points of every person. Kara acknowledges Tom is sensitive to critique, and while she doesn't bite her tongue and hold off on issues that annoy her, she's intentionally responsive to the way she expresses her complaints so as not to worsen Tom's wounds.

Tom also recognizes that Kara is prone to feeling ignored or thrown aside. He understands that this is not about him, but about her, her upbringing, and wiring, and while she's communicating to him, he makes an attempt to react instantly because he knows it's important to her. And he's not feeling resentful for doing so because he doesn't feel like he's caving into a desire, but is instead being considerate for her feelings.

In developing a trustworthy relationship, understanding what your spouse is sensitive to, and promising to try your utmost to stop walking into each other's emotional potholes, goes a long way. What you don't want to do is to ignore the sensitivities of the other or disagree over which fact is right. Everybody has at least one emotional wound, so as a person, you need to speak about these issues easily, so uncover them and respond empathetically.

The dilemma is because once again, you don't — because the general interaction is so minimal and compromised because you can't have these discussions — or that both of you couldn't work it out and let each other know what you really want.

4. Do you talk about the future? Are you on the same page about vision and goals?

This is a problem which has two aspects. It's about having a shared vision about what's relevant in life — children and family; work and career, money — and what that allows for a successful life. And it's about vision, really: how do you envision your ideal day or your ideal life? What are your priorities, and what is your purpose? Can you be constructive, personally, and as a couple to think ahead to figure out what happens to you both?

Yet, once again, integrity is ingrained in these conversations: while your priorities and vision can evolve with time, can you convey your aspirations and expectations without fear of criticism? May you ask what is important to you, and do you agree?

5. Are you compatible as a couple regarding individual vs. couple time?

It's your expectations, wishes, and perceptions about how you're still spending your time. Do I want us to settle down on the sofa and watch television together at night, or are you doing things with the kids when I am doing tasks or doing some work? Is it okay that you hang out with your mates on Saturday or play soccer with your kids, or that I practice my oboe every night for an hour without you feeling guilty or deprived?

Again, communication is an obstacle here, but there is still a consensus on what each of you envisages and wants for time together and as a couple.

6. Are you compatible with the needs of affection and sex?

Although that too can evolve with time, are you both on it as a front-end problem in the same range? This is about libido but also what you need to feel attached to each other. If one still feels sexually oppressed or the other always under threat, it easily leads to a struggle for control. Again, the secret to clarity, the willingness to say what each wants without disintegrating into a confrontation or power struggle.

7. Are you compatible with work?

Since work is such an essential part of the life of each person, it is essential that you are on the same page, so that you can be cooperative. When Kara decides to throw herself into her career and is often able to work 12 hours a day or Tom chooses to take income out of the mutual bank plan to launch his own company, is it all right? On the other side, if Kara sees a career as just work, isn't involved in busting to step up the corporate ladder and would just take less salary with less hassle and more time off, is that all right?

Obviously, this is not simply about the job itself but its effect on leisure, personal life, money — that is, priorities.

8. Are you in agreement about the role of the extended family?

Was it reasonable for my mom to come over every Sunday for brunch, or that we travel every Christmas to visit my friends, or that I owe my brother money to pay his lawyer to finalize his divorce?

It is about combining social traditions and aspirations — all about fixing problems. Perhaps your mother can come for dinner, but not every week; we ought to rotate Christmas between our families; you may lend money to your brother, but there will be a limit on it that we all accept.

9. Do you get along with your in-laws?

Another aspect is the assumptions for the extent of involvement, watching them during those Sundays or holidays, and getting to drink excessively before, during, and after that is another. When it's impossible to move together, so why? Perhaps your mother-in-law offers so much guidance, or is your sister-in-law a bit of a drama queen who has always been known to suck out the room's oxygen?

Once, can you communicate your feelings to your spouse, will he or you give the mother-in-law or sister any positive input without being upsetting any of them?

10. Is your partner, your best friend? Do you feel emotionally safe with him? Do you feel that she always has your back that you can always go to her for help?

Perhaps those are the most critical issues. The thread that flows through both of these queries is around the method being consistent with core problems — the content — but also, more importantly, how you're addressing them. If you both feel comfortable and know your partner is in your corner, you will find a way to sort out all the other problems — the stuff. But if not, why not? It is the large boulder halfway through the lane. This is where, if temporarily, any additional professional support will offer a comfortable space to chat about such things, to let someone raise the concerns that are too complicated to raise yourself.

Yet that's also where you need to find the confidence — to figure out how you truly feel, describe your own goals and dreams, and decide what you need most.

Chapter 05: Strategies to Overcome Anxiety, Negativity, and Jealousy in a Relationship

This chapter will help you to cope with the anxiety, negativity and jealousy in a relationship. Easy to follow strategies are discussed so that the relationship can survive for a life time.

5.1 Overcoming Anxiety

People with lower self-esteem have more anxiety regarding relationships, which may discourage them from enjoying the rewards of a loving relationship. Individuals with low self-esteem not only expect their spouse to view them in a positive light than they perceive themselves, but they have difficulty even remembering their partner's affirmations at times of self-doubt. Furthermore, acting out of our anxieties will drive away a partner, thereby creating a prophecy which fulfills itself. Since this battle is internal and goes on most of the time, irrespective of situations, it's crucial to tackle our anxieties without distorting or pulling our spouse into them. We can achieve so in two steps:

- Discover the real causes of anxiety.

- Fight an internal adversary who is sabotaging the relationship.

Where does our anxiety come from?

Nothing awakens distant hurts like an emotional connection. Our relationships have more than anything else, evoked old memories from our experience. And in all cases, our minds are filled with the same neurochemicals.

We all have functioning models for relationships that were developed with powerful caretakers in our early attachments. Our early behavior will affect our relationships with adults. Our style of attachment determines which partners we chose and the complexities that play out in our relations. A stable pattern of connection makes one individual feel more relaxed and self-possessed. However, if anyone has an anxious or concerned type of relationship, they may be more prone to feel anxious about their mate.

It is important to learn the relationship type, as it will allow us to understand that we can replicate a pattern from our experience. This will help us select better spouses and shape stronger partnerships and, in effect, will improve our type of connection. Finally, it will make us more mindful of how our feelings of anxiety, centered on the old as compared to our present condition, can be distorted.

The anxieties can often derive from a "powerful inner voice" we have internalized, relying on the previous harmful practice. For starters, if we have a father who despised himself or who guided negative attitudes against us, we continue to internalize the point of view and hold it within our heads like a mean coach. This inner critic appears to be very outspoken regarding issues like our relationships, which really matter to us. Next, the vital inner voice sparked suspicions regarding the value the partner had in him, and instead, it turned on him. The second, through the lens of his sensitive inner voice, he interpreted the circumstance, which told him his girlfriend was walking away, his mind filled with horrible thoughts about him. He was only fine one minute. He was listening to an imaginary voice the next minute, showing him all the reasons he couldn't match up, that he'd been dismissed.

Relationships are shaking. They test our fundamental feelings about ourselves and push us out of longlived comfort zones. We continue to turn our inner voice intensity on and reopen old wounds from our experience. When we feel rejected as a child, a romantic partner's aloof conduct is not only going to seem like an utter annoyance. It has the power to take us back to the mental condition of a frightened infant who wanted protection from our mom. As daunting as it can feel to align our contemporary responses with early-life values, habits, and perceptions, it is an important resource for getting to know ourselves and eventually questioning patterns that don't reflect us or really suit our true, adult existence.

How to Deal With Relationship Anxiety

To question our anxiety, we need to get to know our vital voice inside first. Through time it comes into our minds, we will try to grab it. It can be simple, sometimes. We get dressed up to go out on a date, and it says, "You look horrible! You're all too fat. Just cover up on yourself. He's never going to get closer to you. "Other moments, it's going to be more subtle, even relaxing," just keep it to yourself. Don't intervene or show her how you feel so you won't get hurt. "In terms that make us even more anxious, this voice might also turn on our partner," You can't trust him. He's obviously cheating on you! "The first move to questioning the vital inner voice is to recognize it. You can read concrete measures here that you should follow to overcome this inner enemy and keep him from infiltrating your life of love.

When we continue to question these destructive perceptions towards ourselves, we will still aim to take behavior that runs contrary to the guidance of our vital inner mind. This implies, in terms of a relationship, not acting out on the grounds of unwarranted insecurities or behaving in ways we do not value. Here are a few helpful steps:

Maintain your independence.

Keeping a perception of ourselves apart from our spouse is important. The goal of a relationship should be to make a fruit salad and not a smoothie. In other terms, we shouldn't overlook important pieces of who we are to merge into a partner. Rather, anyone of us will strive to preserve the special facets of ourselves that first drew us to each other, even as we step forward. Growing of us should stay firm in this way, recognizing that we are a complete being in and of ourselves.

Don't overreact, no matter how anxious you are.

It's better said than done, of course, but we all know it our anxieties will catalyze some pretty damaging actions. Jealous or possessive actions will harm our partner, not to mention ourselves. Calling every few minutes, snooping through their text messages to see where they are and what are they up to, growing angry every time they smile at some beautiful person — these are all actions we can resist no matter how nervous it makes us because, in the end, we'll be much better and more comfortable. What is more, we should be trustworthy.

Since we can only alter our half of the dynamic, it's also worth talking about whether there are any acts we do that drive away our mate. When we behave in a manner that we appreciate and yet don't feel that we deserve what we want, we should make a deliberate effort to speak to our partner about it or alter the scenario, so we never have to feel betrayed or encourage ourselves to act in ways that we don't appreciate.

Don't seek reassurance.

Running to our companion to comfort us while we feel anxious contributes only to more vulnerability. Note, these habits arise from inside us, and it doesn't matter how clever, beautiful, respectable, or desirable our companion assures us we are until we can conquer them inside ourselves. We will aspire to feel good inside ourselves, no matter what. That implies embracing completely the love and devotion that our spouse is steering towards us. Yet it doesn't imply turning at our companion for reassurance at any level to ensure we're all right, a pressure it falls on our spouse and detracts from ourselves.

Stop measuring.

It is essential that we do not continuously analyze or test any step our spouse makes. We must recognize that our companion is a different sovereign minded individual. We're not all going to see it the same way or show our feelings the same way. This doesn't suggest that we would settle for somebody that doesn't give us everything we want in a partnership, so once we meet anyone we respect and enjoy, we will strive not to get into a system of tit-for-tat in which we continuously calculate that owes what and when.

In terms of sophistication and sharing of goodwill, a relationship would be fair. We should clearly express what we want if things sound wrong, but we do not ask our companion to read our minds or precisely know what to do all the time. When we fall into the blame game, it's a difficult loop to break away from.

Go all in.

We all have anxiety, but by remaining honest to ourselves, we will increase our openness to the multiple ambiguities that a growing relationship eventually poses. We should invest in a person even though we know that they have the potential to do us damage. Holding one foot out of the door just holds the relationship as tight as it may and can destroy it entirely. If we encourage ourselves to be cherished and be accepted, then we are required to feel anxious as well, but keeping it out has more benefits than we can think. When we take a gamble without letting our anxieties influence our actions, the best-case scenario is that the relationship is blossoming, and the worst case is that we are growing inside ourselves. There is no lack of time that has told us much about ourselves or helped nourish our capacity to love and be insecure.

5.2 Overcoming Negativity

Negativity in relationships causes conflicts between couples such as violence, abandonment, infidelity, lack of trust, etc. They both lack interest for each other and the relationship, leaving their future ambiguous as a couple.

Neglecting your Partner

The most significant aspect of a relationship is the development of companionship and being around with one another. Once we start offering our attention to other hobbies and desires than our partner, this gives rise to problems of neglect, which may trigger ups and downs in the relationship.

Not Being Attentive Towards your Partner

It is not enough to be present there. If there are no feelings in it, the relationship does not last. To be there, also be able to express your affection and respect for your partner. Tell yourself in both physical and emotional ways.

Being Dishonest

Those five letters T-R-U-S-T describe the base of your relationship. In every relation, it is the most important element. Lying and infidelity destroys the bond between two people. Cheating will create significant complications, so partners are encouraged to consult in order to navigate through this season.

Physical Abuse

Aggressive behavior is never appropriate, especially when the interaction contributes to abuse. Physical, mental, or sexual violence destroys relationships and families and in relationships gives rise to toxic energies. Ensure that the toxic partner is involved in conflict management programs. And if the behavior does not improve, it is easier to withdraw from this relationship.

Gossiping

It's good to chat about your marriage issues with your mates and family, whether you still explore the solutions. Yet if it's a mere conversation, then it's considered a gossip that gives marriage negativity. Your wife might felt cheated, for example, that you leaked confidential and intimate details to others. Your partner may even find gossiping an emotional scam.

Putting Yourself Last

Nice Guys Also End Last "is a phrase that has started to make a lot of sense for the men and women who are committed. Martyrs are uncommon individuals, and they are always furious, resentful, and disappointed. It does not mean to be inconsiderate and show no concerns for others. When you wish to live and develop a good relationship, so you do need to fulfill your needs. Make sure you are viewed with dignity by people if you function like a doormat, you encourage hostility in your relationship. Stand up for yourself, and protest if you feel disrespectful. Respect yourself almost as much as your spouse does.

10 Ways to keep negativity away from Your Relationships

1. Have Open Lines Of Communication.

Healthy partnerships need direct, uninhibited communication; if the people in it hold secrets and shut themselves off having actual discussions, no relationship will last for long. Relationships will take a turn for the worst easily if people start distancing themselves and will not accept that the other person has done anything or said anything to annoy them. Nonetheless, when you threaten somebody, you will always respond rationally and hold a civilized dialog that doesn't result in screaming and shouting at each other's names.

Only note that a good relationship is founded on honesty and clear communication, and if you want to prevent conflict, seek to foster both in all your close relationships.

2. Don't Pick Apart the Other Person's Flaws.

A sure-fire way to begin disputes and wreck a relationship is to nit-pick and put somebody's imperfections in their face. Note that each individual may have attributes under the skin, but such attributes will not make up the entirety of who they are. Bear in mind, though, that you certainly have characteristics that bother some people, but your near friends and family might not find it a point to blame you about them. They embrace you exactly the way you are, the defects, and all.

When you don't particularly like the company of someone, you should let the relationship go without tearing down the other individual – just come clean to them and reassure them tactfully that you think it will help all of you to go your separate ways.

3. Appreciate One Another.

If it's your co-worker, partner, relative, mom, or dad, let the individual realize that from time to time, you appreciate them. Everybody in life deserves to feel valued, and then they feel like they've made a difference in this world. If you consider and compliment somebody's good qualities, they would be motivated to perceive you in the same way.

Optimistic relationships require both partners to have affection, commitment, and reciprocal respect. Every time you see your mate, your co-worker, your family, and so forth, let them realize that you love them and how much you truly respect them.

4. Don't Hold Onto Relationship Grudges.

Everyone is making mistakes, so that doesn't mean they need to be kept above their heads for their entire lives. Accept that from time to time, humans make errors, and forgive the individual for the mishap. Of course, if someone wanted to harm you deliberately, you would need to handle it a little differently, but most people don't go out of their way to inflict another person's pain. It was actually just an innocent error because, at some stage, no person on Earth would really go through their whole lives without messing up.

Know you have made errors in the past, too, so you will not like anyone to continually remind you of your shortcomings too.

5. Leave Jealousy At The Door.

Everybody in life has a specific direction, and some may appear to have more or do better than you do. That doesn't suggest you can equate yourself to them and feel bad simply because everything you haven't accomplished has been achieved by them. What about the race you finished up without your friend? What about the holidays you took a couple of years earlier that your friends asked you they had dreamed about taking?

Don't let jealousy take control of you, for it will deprive you of pleasure and influence your judgments. Bear in mind all of the great interactions and successes that might not be under your belt – that can help put everything in perspective and make you happier with others rather than envy them.

6. Don't Fall Into The destructive Habit of Complaining.

Many people view their time together as an excuse for throwing all their life problems onto each other and dissipating their grievances. After the encounter, this leaves both individuals feeling exhausted and uninspired, which opens the way for further conflict in the future. Instead of arguing about issues, think about alternatives.

Note the good stuff in life, and pick one another up. Healthy relationships are perfect when both people feel happier, rather than bitter.

7. Don't Compare Your Relationship To Others.

Every relationship is unique and beautiful; the relationship with your buddy would look different from the relationship with anyone else, so enjoy it for what it is. When you just crave what you don't have, you can never have good relationships and respecting the wonderful bond you share.

8. Don't Try To Change People.

Respect people at this moment for whoever they are, rather than coercing them to adjust for your own gain. People will only improve if they want to, so just concentrate on what you value about them, rather than blaming them for their flaws. If they believe you in having to adjust, you may kindly find out a direction for them to improve, but don't take it upon yourself to mandate that they do.

9. Bring Kindness To The Relationship.

They would be more likely to demonstrate caring and affection for you if you express love for the other person. Be one like what you expect to see in the world, and your relationship will thrive because you will draw others with the same passion that you already do.

10. Laugh More.

If you have plenty to laugh about, it's hard to be pessimistic, so share jokes or go on a lovely holiday with family, mates, colleagues, or your partner. Allow your inner kid to come out and play in the midst of life's seriousness, then not only do you become more light-hearted and happy, but the fun will also put you back together and disperse stress.

5.3 Overcoming Jealousy

How to Deal with Jealousy

No-one wants to be jealous. But jealousy is an inherent feeling that can be felt in every single one of us. The trouble with jealousy is not that from time to time, it shows up, nor what it brings to us when we don't get hold of it. Experiencing what occurs when we enable our jealousy to overtake us or influence the way we feel about ourselves and everyone around us may be terrifying. This is why knowing where our competitive emotions really come from and discovering how to cope with jealousy in positive, constructive ways is key to so many facets of our lives, from our intimate interactions to our jobs to our personal ambitions.

Why are we so jealous, then?

Research has shown predictably, that increased jealousy correlates with lower self-esteem. "Most of us are still oblivious of the underlying guilt that resides inside us, for it comes too easily to speak of ourselves with self-critical feelings. Yet the degree to which we feel jealous and insecure in the present can be heavily influenced by guilt from our experience. The 'critical voice inside' is a type of negative selftalk. This perpetuates negative thoughts and emotions, with intense attention pushing us to evaluate, measure, and judge ourselves (and also others). This is one explanation of why it's so important to know how to cope with jealousy.

This voice will intensify our feelings of jealousy with negative and malicious comments flooding our minds. In reality, what our vital inner voice informs us regarding our condition is always more complicated to deal with than the actual circumstance. A rejection or alienation by our mate is hard, but all the horrible stuff our sensitive inner voice informs us about ourselves after the incident is what really pains us even more. "You're such an insane person. Have you ever felt you should truly be happy? "You're going to end up lonely. You can never trust someone again. "Take a deeper look at two forms of jealousy to explain how this inner adversary fuels our bad emotions about jealousy: romantic jealousy and competitive jealousy. Although these two types of jealousy sometimes intersect, individually understanding them can help us understand better how jealous feelings can influence various areas of our lives, and how we can best cope with jealousy.

Romantic Jealousy

It is a simple fact that relationships get better because individuals don't get unnecessarily jealous. The longer that we will hang onto our jealous emotions and make sense of them apart from our mate, the happier we would be. Note, our jealousy also stems from our own fear – a sense that we are destined to be betrayed, harmed, or rejected. Unless we cope with this feeling inside ourselves, in every relationship, no matter what the circumstances, we are likely to fall prey to feelings of jealousy, mistrust, or insecurity.

Such pessimistic thoughts towards ourselves derive from very early life experiences. We also bear upon ourselves emotions that our parents or significant relatives have towards us or against themselves. In our current relationships, then, unintentionally, we repeat, reconstruct, or respond to old, familiar dynamics. For instance, if we felt set out as children, we might easily interpret our spouse as dismissing us. We may select a spouse who is more difficult or even adhere to actions that will drive away our spouse.

The degree to which we, as adolescents, inherited self-critical attitudes also affects how much our critical inner voice can influence us in our adult lives, particularly in our relations. And, no matter what our particular perceptions maybe, to some degree, we all hold this inner criticism. Most of us can contribute to bringing a sensation that we are not going to be chosen. The degree to which we think this insecurity impacts the way we feel insecure in a relationship.

Lurking behind the anger towards our spouses or questioning a perceived danger from third entities are also serious thoughts about ourselves. Thoughts saying, "what is he seeing in her?' Can easily transform into' She is so much more pretty / thinner / successful than I am! 'Even as our worst suspicions come to life when we hear about the affair of a spouse, we always respond by turning frustration to ourselves as being 'foolish, unlovable, destroyed, or unwelcome.' Like a sadistic teacher, our vital inner voice warns us not to trust or feel too weak. It tells us that we are not lovable and that we are not fit for romance. It is the soft whisper which spreads cynicism, distrust, and confusion. "Why would she work tardy? "Why does he prefer over me his friends? "What does she do while I'm away? "Why is it that he gives too much attention to what she says? "Those of us who are acquainted with how jealousy functions realize that far too frequently such feelings gradually tend to sprout and blossom into even bigger, more entrenched assaults on oneself and/or our partner. "She's trying to hang around you. Somebody else has to be there." "He is losing interest. He wants to run away from you." "Who will listen? You are too dull. "At some stage in a relationship, this insecure feeling will emerge, from the first date to the twentieth year of a marriage. We listen to our inner critic in an effort to defend ourselves and step back from being close to our spouse. And we still seem to be more competitive of an absolute trap after we've withdrawn from doing what we want. If we realize at any level that we don't consider our relationship a focus or consciously follow our aim of being near or caring, we continue to feel more vulnerable and jealous. That's why knowing how to cope with jealousy is much more relevant, and not acting unconsciously on jealous feelings by driving our spouse farther apart.

Competitive Jealousy

Although it can sound futile or illogical, having what others have and feeling jealous is totally normal. Whether we interpret those emotions, though, is quite important to our fulfillment and enjoyment point. This is simply a negative trend of demoralizing consequences because we use these emotions to support our inner rivals, to break down ourselves or others. However, if we don't encourage such emotions to fall through the hands of our vital inner voice, we will potentially use them to understand what we desire, to be more goal-driven, or just to experience more self-acceptance of what influences us.

It's all right, also positive, to let ourselves have a competitive mind-set. It can feel amazing when we just let ourselves get the momentary sensation without any decision or action plan. But, if we ruminate or distort this thinking into a self-criticism or an assault on another human, we get hurt at it. If we consider ourselves being overreacted or plagued by our thoughts of jealousy, we should do a few things.

Be aware of what gets triggered.

Think of the different things that make you feel worked up. Is it a friend who has financial success? An ex-partner who dates someone else? A friend who speaks her mind in meetings?

Ask yourself for what critical inner voices come up.

What kinds of thoughts spark the competitive feelings? Are you using the jealous emotions to bring yourself down? Do they make you feel weak, incompetent, ineffective, etc.? Is there a sequence or pattern that seems familiar to those thoughts?

Ponder about the deeper implications and origins of these thoughts.

Do you sense a certain urgency to get something done? Is there something that you think you should be? What does that entail for you obtaining this thing? Does that refer to your past?

When we have asked these questions to ourselves, we may appreciate how such emotions may have more to do with unresolved problems inside ourselves than with our current life or the individual; our jealousy is aimed at. For ourselves, we should show more patience and seek to abandon the prejudices that cause us to feel unhappy.

How to Stop Being a Jealous Companion

If you let jealousy go unregulated, the relationship would decline. It needs trust for yourself and your partner to realize how to avoid being a competitive wife or husband. Get to the root of your jealousy and build a more healthy relationship.

Be honest about jealousy's impact.

You can't fix a dilemma because you refuse to consider it. Be real, instead of claiming that you are not jealous, or that your jealousy is not a problem. How are you feeling, and how are they affecting your relationship because of your insecurities?

Recognizing the issues that your jealousy is creating might be complicated, but take pride in the fact that you are making the first move towards a stronger relationship.

Ask what your jealousy is telling you.

Instead of seeing jealousy as a problem, see your jealousy as a solution. Jealousy (or some other query about relationships) is a window of insight that we should gaze into and achieve clarification. Instead of turning off the jealous behavior right away, seek first to grasp the behavior. What issue is the jealousy attempt to overcome? If you feel jealous that your companion has violated your trust, perhaps the real issue is the lack of trust. It is your insecurities that require consideration if you pass your insecurities into your spouse. If you feel jealous of the achievements of your partner, maybe there is an inappropriate competitive aspect that needs to be removed.

Whatever the source, it can help you get to the root of how to avoid getting jealous in a relationship by looking at jealousy as a "solution" and going back from there. To find permanent relief, you will fix it by moving to the real issue.

List your insecurities.

Looking at yourself begins by learning how to avoid being a jealous husband or wife. What sort of fear causes your jealousy? Is it because of perfectionism you are uncertain of yourself? Would you equate yourself to other people? You don't make this statement yourself to blame-you own your part in the relationship.

Cultivate self-confidence.

If you have worked up a list of the insecurities that cause your jealousy, write down a solution for each one of them-. When you remain in the shadow of an ex-partner, make a compilation of all the qualities that your spouse likes in you. If you are always contrasting yourself to celebrities, unfollow them for a week on Instagram. You'll be able to build the selfconfidence you need to conquer jealousy by allowing yourself space from feelings of inferiority.

Consider the source of your insecurity.

Mastering how to avoid jealousy in a relationship is also a question of treating past wounds. If you deal with jealousy because of an underlying condition such as childhood abuse or addiction, get the help you need to tackle it. You will turn your conflicts into sources of power with the right support.

Be honest with your partner.

When you are dealing with jealousy, your partner has undoubtedly recognized it too. Most likely, your partner will also help the situation. Through actively collaborating, you appreciate your commitment when keeping your partner committed as well – and offer them the chance to help you while you seek for a solution.

Build healthy coping skills.

Even in a relationship, it can be difficult to let go of jealousy if you don't have a more positive way to connect. If your partner does not give you a justification to feel paranoid or jealous (i.e., by cheating on you or lying frequently), it is up to you to suppress your jealousy trigger. Recognize you don't need to feel jealous – you're already used to that. Care for yourself to nurture your physical,

emotional, and mental wellbeing. These become the routine as you emphasize positive coping strategies, which ultimately eliminate jealousy.

Dissolving the feelings of rage and jealousy in relationships requires shifting the underlying values about fear and unconscious expectations about what the mate is doing.

The steps to completely end jealous reactions are:

Recovering emotional influence so you can regain charge of your thoughts to stop reactive behavior.

Shift your point of view, so that in your mind you may move back from the plot. This should allow you a time span to stop a jealous or angry response to do something else.

Identify the core beliefs which activate the emotional response.

Be mindful that your mental convictions aren't valid. That is distinct from scientifically "knowing" that the tales are not real.

Establish the power of your concentration, and you can choose deliberately which tale is unfolding through your subconscious and which feelings you experience.

There are a number of elements that establish the jealousy dynamics. As such, successful approaches would have to tackle various aspects of values, opinions, desires, and the will power. When you skip one or more of these factors, then you leave the path open to revert to certain negative feelings and behaviors.

You will move back from the narrative by doing a few basic exercises, which project the mind and withdraw from the emotional response. When you just want to alter your thoughts and behavior, only you should achieve it. Training valuable knowledge requires only the desire. You can find useful techniques and activities to conquer the internal jealousy response.

Principle envy factors are assumptions that cause feelings of anxiety Feelings of low self-esteem are centered on perceptions that we have in a conceptual picture of who we are. We don't have to adjust to remove the fear and low self-esteem; we only have to shift our confidence in the delusional self-image. While certain may believe that this may be tough, it is just daunting because most may not have acquired the requisite skills to alter a conviction. When you learn the techniques, you realize it requires very little time to alter a conviction. You just avoid involving yourself in the tale. It needs more time to believe something than not to believe it.

Chapter 06: Problems and their Solution in Relationship

Everything comes with its own problems that can be solved if dealt carefully and tactically. This chapter will enlighten about the most common problems and their solutions in a relationship.

6.1 Problems with Solutions That Can Save a Relationship

It is the unusual couple not crashing into a number of bumps in the lane. However, if you know in advance what such relationship concerns maybe, you'll have a much greater opportunity to move through them.

And if any relationship has its ups and downs, committed spouses have known how to handle the challenges to maintain their romantic life alive. They're hanging in there, solving problems, and discovering how to navigate with the complicated daily issues. Others accomplish so by reading books and blogs on self-help, attending lectures, going to therapy, watching certain positive individuals, or even use trial and error.

6.2 Relationship Problem: Communication

All issues related to relationships arise from inadequate contact. You can't interact when searching your cell phone, viewing television, or scrolling through the segment on sports.

Problem-solving strategies:

- Make a close encounter with each other. If you reside together, put your mobile phones on silent mode, put the kids to bed and let the calls pick up via voicemail.

- If you cannot "communicate" without raising your voices, head to a quiet place like a library, a park, or a restaurant where you'd be ashamed to see someone shouting you.

- Set up guidelines. Seek not to disrupt before the partner talks, or forbid phrases like "You still ..." or "You never...."

- Use body gestures to indicate you are attentive. Do not doodle, check your phone, or pick your nails. Nod, so the other individual understands you're getting the word, and if you need to, rephrase it.

Of starters, claim, "What I hear you claim is you seem like you have more responsibilities at home, even though we both work." Whether you're correct, the other will clarify. If what the other individual actually said was, "Yeah, you're a slob, so, by trying to tidy up after you, you generate more stress for me," he or she might tell it, albeit in a polite way.

6.3 Relationship Problem: Sex

Also, couples who love one another, sexually, maybe a mismatch. Such issues are compounded by a lack of sexual self-confidence and knowledge. Yet having intercourse is one of the last aspects that you need to quit. Sex puts partners back together, stimulates hormones that support the bodies both mentally and physically, and maintains a happy couple's chemistry alive.

Problem-solving strategies:

- Prepare and schedule. Decide on a date, but not when someone is tired, not even at night. Maybe during the baby's afternoon nap or a "before-work quickie." Ask friends or relatives to take the children for a sleepover every other Friday night. "When sex is on the list, it enhances the excitement. Turning it up, a little will even make sex more enjoyable. Why not have sex in the kitchen? Or by the fire? Or standing up in the lobby?

- Know what actually makes you and the partner come up with a specific Sexy List for both of you. Mix the lists and use them to build more situations that turn you both on.

- If the sexual relationship problems can't be resolved on their own, consult an experienced sex therapist to help you both acknowledge and resolve your issues.

6.4 Relationship Problem: Money

Problems with money will begin well before the wedding vows are exchanged. These can derive, for example, from court costs or from a wedding's high cost. People with finance problems should take a deep breath and undergo a meaningful financial discussion.

Problem-solving strategies:

- Be honest with the financial position you are in. If things have gone south, it's impossible to follow the same lifestyle.

- In the heat of combat, do not address the issue. Instead, set out a period that you will consider comfortable and non-threatening.

- Recognize that one spouse is a saver and one a spender, recognize that both have advantages and consent to profit about each other's habits.

- Should not cover refunds or debts. Take tax records to the table, including a current credit check, pay stubs, savings balances, compensation plans, loans, and assets.

- Make no liability.

- Develop a Shared Strategy with savings.

- Decide which individual is liable for paying the bills each month.

- Enable each person to be autonomous by setting aside money at his or her discretion.

- Agree on short and long term goals. Getting specific objectives is good, but you can still have family goals.

- Discuss about caring for your parents when they age, and how to provide for their financial needs when required.

6.5 Relationship Problem: Struggles Over Daily Home Chores

Most of the partners work outside the home and often at more than one job. And it is necessary to split the chores at home equally.

Problem-solving strategies:

- Plan your tasks and be specific about your respective chores. "Write down all the work and decide who is doing what." Be honest, and no frustration builds up.

- Stay open to alternatives. When you both dislike housework, you may be willing to pay for a cleaning service. When one of you enjoys housework, you should do the washing and yard for the other person. You should be imaginative to take into consideration desires — as long as it sounds appropriate to all of you.

6.6 Relationship Problem: Not prioritizing your relationship

If you want to maintain your romantic life alive, you cannot leave your relationship as a focal point when you say, "I do." "Relationships lack their luster. Make yours a mission to Find It, Keep It, and Make It Last."

Problem-solving strategies:

- Do the stuff you used to do when you first dated: express your gratitude, praise each other, keep in contact with each other during the day, and demonstrate your curiosity.

- Date night's preparation. Schedule time on the calendar, much like you should for every other significant thing of your existence.

- Show reverence for one another. Say "thank you" and "I love ..." This will let your spouse realize they're significant.

6.7 Relationship Problem: Conflict

Occasional conflict is a normal part of life. But if you and your wife sound like you're acting in your own horror interpretation of the Groundhog Day movie — i.e., keep experiencing the same crappy scenarios day after day — it's time to break away from this dysfunctional ritual. You will lessen the rage as you take the initiative, and have a rational look at the root problems.

Problem-solving strategies:

You and your companion will learn to fight in a more social, supportive manner. In this relationship, make certain tactics part of who you are.

- You know that you're not a survivor. Whether you respond and how you respond is your preference.

- Be honest with yourself. When you're in the midst of a dispute, are your responses directed to settling the issue, or are you eager for payback? When the remarks are hurtful and blameless, it is better to take a deep breath and change the tactic.

- Turn it up. If you choose to act in the way that has brought you past pain and unhappiness, this time, you cannot anticipate another outcome. One slight change alone will make a huge difference. Hold back for a couple of minutes, because you normally run straight in to protect yourself until your partner's done chatting. You'll be shocked how only a slight tempo change will alter the entire essence of the statement.

- Give a few; get a bunch. If you're mistaken, apologize. Sure it's challenging, but just try and watch something amazing happen.

You can't regulate the actions of someone else. You have the charge of yourself only.

6.8 Relationship Problem: Trust

Trust is an integral part of a bond. Do you see any stuff that can lead you to not trust your partner? And are you having unresolved problems that keep you from trusting each other?

Problem-solving strategies:

Through pursuing certain guidelines, you and your partner will develop trust in each other.

- Stick to the commitments.

- Be punctual.

- Do whatever you say you're going to do.

- Don't lie to your partner or to anyone — not just tiny white lies.

- Be honest, even when arguing.

- Be sensitive to the feelings of others. You may also differ, so don't underestimate how you feel towards your mate.

- Call, if you say you're going to.

- Call your spouse and tell you're going to come home late.

- Keep the workload in equal proportion.

- If things go badly, don't overreact.

- Never say anything that you are unable to take back.

- Don't dig into painful wounds.

- Honour the boundaries of your mate.

- Do not be jealous.

- Be a Great listener.

While there would still be conflicts in a relationship, you will always do things to mitigate marital concerns, if not prevent them entirely.

Let's be practical first. It's a Movie dream to believe that your partner would fulfill all your desires — and should be able to resolve these issues out without thinking. "Ask for what you need first. Then, use entertainment — try to let stuff go and love each other more. Ultimately, be able to focus on the relationship and just look at what has to be accomplished. Don't presume it will be different for anyone else. Unless you cope with issues, there would always be the same lack of abilities that get in the way today will still trigger difficulties no matter what relationship you have.

Chapter 07: What a Healthy Relation looks like?

This chapter will let you know and learn that what a healthy relationship is and what strategies to follow for a healthy relationship. These are simple and easy to practice for a better and stronger relationship.

7.1 Talking Openly

Communication is an integral aspect of a stable relationship. Healthy couples find time for a regular check-in with each other. It's important to speak more than just about parenting and household maintenance. Seek to spend a few minutes each day exploring deeper or more intimate issues in order to stay committed to your spouse in the long term.

That doesn't say you can stop taking up difficult topics. Holding anxieties or problems to oneself will generate resentment. However, it helps to be polite when arguing difficult topics. Research indicates that the way you interact with your spouse is significant, and the negative impact of communication may have a negative impact on the bond.

Disagreements are part of any relationship. However, some types of combat are particularly harmful. Couples that use disruptive tactics during conflicts —

such as shouting, resorting to personal attacks, or withdrawing from the debate — are more likely to split up than couples that clash constructively. To cope with conflicts, use positive approaches such as listening to the point of view of the spouse, and respecting their concerns is a better path forward.

Keeping it interesting

It may be challenging to remain close to your spouse or be romantic between children, jobs, and outside obligations.

Many people schedule daily date nights to make things fun. Nevertheless, even dates will get stale if you still watch a movie or go to the same restaurant. Experts advocate stopping the norm and doing fresh things — whether it's dance, attending a class together, or planning a picnic afternoon.

When should couples seek help?

Every relationship has ups and downs, so certain variables in a relationship are more prone to cause bumps than others. For starters, finance and parenting decisions cause ongoing disputes. One indication of a dilemma is repetitive iterations of the same clash again and again. Psychologists may help partners strengthen trust in these situations, and find healthier strategies to step past the dispute.

You don't have to wait until there are indicators of problems in a relationship until you try to improve the alliance. Marital education programs that help to learn skills such as good communication, effective listening, and conflict management have been shown to reduce divorce risk.

Know more about your partner

How much does your partner know you? Do they have the attributes to make you grow into a stronger person? Do the practices that make you think of your relationship twice? Do you know all the positive and negative bits of them?

These are the questions that will make you know whether you are with the right person or not if you are answering. Yet you can always note that not all relationships are flawless, so it is necessary to have an open mind on which imperfections are worth your comprehension.

Here are the important stuff you should learn about your significant other.

Know their Life story – both the good and the bad parts.

Upon first sight, many people believe in love and claim it can be the beginning of something wonderful. Most people, though, learned their lessons the hard way and discovered that love is not enough to keep a relationship going.

You will need other aspects, so one significant reason is to allow your spouse to realize who he/she is – so it doesn't end there. You must also completely embrace what you will find when you unravel the tale of their lives, particularly the bad bits.

Know the Things and habits that annoy them.

Everyone has a list of things that bother them, so it is very helpful to know every detail on your partner's list, and you can make the appropriate changes to prevent the typical trivial fights.

Try to realize as best as possible that you are two separate individuals with very different backgrounds, and reaching a compromise is one step closer to creating a deeper bond, particularly if you're new in the relationship.

Favorite things and people.

Create a list of things and individuals that could make them happy, and find it in your heart to value them as well. This is vital that you are conscious of these essential parts of the existence of your significant other as apart from demonstrating that you are very vigilant. It is a sensitive way to consider the fact that her joy will come from various places – not only from you and your relationship.

The things that fuel their temper.

What's making them angry? Which are the things, incidents, or acts capable of causing them to erupt? Anger is a fairly normal emotion felt by any human being, so knowing what causes it is a helpful way to really learn the other person.

You will gain a lot about the way people convey their frustration as well as reaction to the triggering stuff.

The memories that make them cry.

Understanding grief and how people are keeping painful feelings will help you get to know a person better. By understanding what makes your life's love cry, trying to reach them out, and making that bond, you are building a sanctuary that they will still run to anytime they feel like breaking down.

Know the relationships are not just about love. Beyond being a lover, you're also a mate, a trustworthy confidant, and an ever-supportive partner.

7.9 Their dreams and aspirations.

What are the things they really hoped for? What are the goals and aspirations they set out to pursue? Learn your companion well, and they admire their strength and determination to tackle the future without any uncertainties.

Seeing how your partner sees herself ten or twenty years from now is an amazing thing because it's just a happy feeling when you're with somebody who is not scared of aiming big because dreaming high.

7.10 The jokes that make them laugh out loud.

Humour can play a very important role in relationships because aside from offering other people a pleasant smile, it can be a nice and quick relief from the unjust challenges in life – so make your spouse laugh.

Find out all of her favorite lines, google the funniest stories, learn and go make this very precious person laugh out loud because it doesn't matter if you're awful at it.

7.11 Their frustrations and defeats.

What are the aspects that reminded them that, even though they earn it, people will not always get what they want? Life challenges will bring down even the most hopeful individual, so make sure to be present when it's the turn of your companion to be aware of that.

Enable them to do tasks they never wanted to attempt again just because they struggled the first time. Be a source of motivation and an undying belief that such losses and mistakes would fail to destroy their spirit.

7.12 The list of their favorite food.

This is more likely to be the most undervalued aspect of any relationship, and this needs more credit. How well do you know the favorite food preferences of your partner? What restaurant is their favorite? Are they in love with Japanese cuisine, or are they more like the spice queen and always wanting Indian food? Go ahead and take her to an amazing experience with food as she deserves all the world's real food.

7.13 The people who broke their heart.

Accept their history and other people who have led to the way they currently see the world. It's a required move for your companion to grasp inside and out completely. Be careful, however, and make sure you have an open mind to consider stuff you can't alter. Only reflect on the fact that it took every phase of your partner's life to make her a happier, stronger human.

7.14 The craziest things that they've done.

Also, the most apparently dull individual has a wild side, and this reality brings more spice to the relationship, particularly if you're still on the stage of getting to know each other better. Ask the right questions, and you can discover inside them a secret labyrinth through passage can be opened only to all who have the key to their heart.

7.15 How they see their future with you.

Last but most significantly, you ought to learn whether you are part of the dream of the future with your partner. Five to ten years from now, what is your role?

Would you still speak to each other about your life and how you want to live it with them?

Understanding your partner well and figuring out the issues, attitudes, and activities that lead to how they see the world will make a difference and help the relationship withstand the time check. Ask the right questions then, and don't be scared to hear the answers.

7.2 Be a Good Listener

10 Tips to Be a Good Listener in Your Relationship

"You really can't listen? You've heard this phrase pretty much at least once in your lifetime. Maybe only a couple of you learned that from your partner. Communicating is also an essential cornerstone in a secure and safe relationship, but communicating requires two elements: talking and listening. Talking is a basic thing that everybody does, but this time the emphasis would be on the listening side. Most people are chatting, so only listening a little bit. Yet, what does one do to be a great listener? Don't worry! Ten strategies below are to help you be one:

Listen more often.

Telling yourself how to become a good listener? The number one suggestion is to listen more often. You may be the person that always talks and forgets how to listen. It never hurts to lower one's ego for long enough to lengthen one's endurance and only listen to what your companion has to tell. When you teach yourself to listen most frequently, as you converse with your boyfriend or girlfriend, it should come automatically.

Communication is a two-way street.

Communication, as stated earlier, is not one way: whether one talks the other listens. Those positions are interchanged from time to time. The dispute occurs where certain functions are not at all shared, and only one talks and other listens. Keep in mind that you should know when to stop talking. Effective contact will never be accomplished if two people in a relationship do not routinely exchange such positions.

Drop your phone.

It is important for you to drop your phone while talking to your girlfriend or boyfriend, particularly if this is a significant problem. That means you appreciate the individual talking, and you're all ears on what he or she has to say. This is disrespectful if, during a face to face talk, one continues checking the screen or fiddling with his or her phone. Turn your phone into silent mode to be a better listener, because those emails and notifications can wait.

Don't interrupt.

Another significant note is never disturbing the one talking in order to become a good listen. Be all ears to what he or she is telling, and wait until the person is done, then share your thoughts on the issue. His or her opinion is just as important as yours on the topic. This shows rudeness if the person speaking is disrupted. Often people get so interested in the topic that they keep cutting off other persons if you see yourself related to this, consider holding the horses and making others take turns.

Make eye contact.

Imagine talking to someone who's never gazing at you or staring at something else but you. It is necessary as a successful listener to create and maintain eye contact. It tells your girlfriend or boyfriend you are really concentrated on the subject. You don't have to look someone in the eye to achieve so, depending on the circumstances, only a quick casual glance would do. Setting up eye contact always gives the individual communicating a clear sense that you are really listening.

Look out for subtle hints.

Someone needs to take care of the implicit cues to be a better listener. Often you can wonder why he or she becomes moody afterward for an unexplained cause after having a friendly talk with your partner. Some people also have implicit clues in their expressions, so they don't want to say it clearly. For starters, if your girlfriend communicates that she wants spaghetti for dinner, she might drop hints about it, and if you're not a good listener, you may not be able to pick up those hints. It is necessary for any listener to take note.

Show enthusiasm.

Conversing with someone who demonstrates that he or she is obviously not interested is never a good idea. You can't just lay back and stare at your girlfriend or boyfriend because you want to be a good listener, you have to prove you're excited about it. You may achieve so by starting the dialogue first, whether by searching for opportunities to extend the discussion or by posing questions for follow-up. But if you do not feel like talking, it's best to allow yourself some space and offer your partner a strong message that you're not in the right state to carry an intelligible conversation.

Be patient.

Patience is a virtue and one of the key components of how to become a good listener. To listen, you have to hold a very ample amount of courage within yourself. You'll definitely need it if your partner complains about something that happened in her or his day. Being good at listening helps the individual to take their time to articulate what they want to tell.

If you consider yourself on the restless side, it is highly advised to take deep breaths and set speaking time intervals.

Give a proper response.

You have to be attentive, too, in order to become a better listener. If just one talks, it's not a good conversation because the other either nods or shakes his or her head. If you're a good listener, you'll be able to respond coherently to any question you're being asked, if you listen well. Often a yes or no is not enough to address the subject. Keep an emphasis on participating in the discussion.

Understand what he or she says into the heart.

This is the same as eating, and you can't just consume the meal, you need to digest it, too. You can't just listen to what he or she has to say. You have to take it to heart as well. When your companion mentions something that does trouble him or her, you should be vigilant. For example, when you are asked to do the tasks, don't make him or her repeat him or herself, recall what job you were given. It demonstrates you are not only listening but adapting what you learned about your discussions to your relationship as well.

This requires effort and a lot of courage to become a great listener. You don't have to try to be one, but instead encourage yourself to make such changes little by little, particularly if you're not the kind of individual that's used to listening. Communication operates both ways, and you just have to take the patience to speak and listen.

7.3 Build Trust

Trusting your mate is one of the most important aspects of a relationship because if you want some sort of romantic relationship to endure, you have to focus on its ability to bind and hold together two individuals, whatever may come. Couples in a longterm relationship have now perfected trust's skill or are now trying gradually to sustain it. That is because trust needs to be won over and again, much like affection and admiration, and should be able to survive any storm that falls in its path.

No matter where you are along this continuum below are few things you can remember:

First, trust in your own worth.

When you want to be a human worthy of trusting others, you have to conquer the deepest insecurities. You have to accept that you are good enough for the one you love, that you are worth their time and energy, and this is when you build the courage to invest in their dedication.

In other terms, the first step you need to take is confidence in yourself and believing in your own value.

Have faith in a partner's love for you.

Second, you ought to feel you're deserving of being cherished. Have faith in the love of your spouse for you, for this is where true confidence occurs. There should be no space for uncertainty and confusion, no place for suspicions and paranoia if you trust in them and how they feel towards you. Building trust in your relationship requires developing a deep and true love for one another.

Value honesty and take time to listen.

Communicate regularly and do your part by being an open speaker and a good listener to get engaged in the discussion. Through building this sanctuary of integrity and transparency, each of you will share your inner thoughts without a doubt and without fear of judgment. Some of the best relationships are founded on integrity and reality principles; just make sure you do it correctly.

Talk about the things that matter.

You must not hesitate to point out concerns and problems which could spoil the relationship. It's all right to be dismissive of your companion and how they play their role, but you shouldn't ignore your own shortcomings too. Maintain and develop trust in your relationship by possessing the confidence to speak about the issues that matter and not be ashamed to accept when mistakes are made.

Be courageous enough not to give in to temptations.

You have to be courageous to reject and withstand the temptations. Know these fleeting distractions are not going to fix anything. Rather, after all, the repercussions of your acts will make their way into your relationship. Your companion can forgive you, but don't expect them to give you the same trust they once had before your heart shattered. They don't deserve the lies, and definitely, they don't deserve the heartaches that come with them.

Resolve relationship issues together.

Trust the relationship and both of the abilities to work together to fix the problems. You should not let other people determine about you both and never let them tell you what to do. Having the ability to restore something that is wrong is an indicator that you can be trusted to be the strength and refuge of your partner in your relationship, particularly during the darkest days.

Don't be scared to ask questions.

One of the best ways to build and retain trust is to enable honesty and integrity to reign at all times – so the only way to enable them to dominate in your relationship is to pose the correct questions without being ashamed of and punished for it. Ask them about the stuff that troubled you a while ago; question your companion about an event that made you feel uncertain about their love for you. You deserve the response. Go ahead, and be courageous.

Be brave enough to hear the truth.

It's also critical that you are strong enough to hear the answers regarding the previous section. Most of the time, reality hurts, but it can set you free too. Your companion may offer you responses that allow you to doubt your love for them, and certain responses might also say something about their feelings towards you. Hearing the facts is so much easier than suffer in silence when you don't realize what is going on exactly.

Never lie in a relationship, no matter how much the truth hurts.

Never lie to anyone if you want someone to trust you – not just if you want to protect them by being hurt. If you want to be genuinely satisfied in your relationship, it is an utter norm. A love tale based on lies can never last – and this experience has been learned by others the hard way, and no matter how hurtful and devastating the reality can be, you have to do it and say it out loud.

Develop a connection beyond romance.

Finally, you will learn to trust your significant other not only as a companion in a relationship, not only as a lover in an intimate relationship but as a friend whom you may indulge in the deepest bits of yourself.

As friends and as two individuals who truly want the best for each other, you must build and maintain trust.

Trust is one of the qualities you can't quickly earn. You must earn it, and you must strive to focus on it every day of your life. Continuously preserving this essential aspect of your relationship may sound stressful, but it's not actually that challenging, as long as you respect honesty as much as you respect, love.

Know, though, that success in a relationship depends not just on how much love you give, but also on significant values such as trust, loyalty, and commitment – and both are equally valuable – so make sure you don't take either of them for granted.

7.4 Be Less Jealous

7 Strategies to Deal with Jealousy in Intimate Relationships

It's natural to feel a little jealous at times when you're in a relationship, particularly if you have really strong feelings for your partner. Occasional jealousy is good and can also bring to the relationship a little bit of enthusiasm and zest. But as this jealousy is more prevalent and severe and often overwhelming, what should be done?

Why Do People Get Jealous?

The typical evolutionary theory of jealousy is that men are terrified of sexual infidelity because they want to be completely confident that their offspring is theirs. Women are more associated with sexual infidelity, as they are worried about the wellbeing of their children and want to make sure their husband loves, cares, and preserves their children.

People are more scared now than ever before of being denied, not welcomed, not respected, and concerned about losing someone they care for. Those experiences of loss are normal. Once again, thoughts and jealousy feelings are serious, and they partially derive from anxiety. If anxiety diminishes, so does jealousy. Here are a few approaches that will help you out if you feel jealous quite often:

1. Don't Act On Your Feelings

It is impossible not to react the way you feel. The sensation of jealousy or some other emotions is not the issue; the true difficulty starts when you decide to act on the jealousy and let it overtake you. You can sense it, so you don't have to act on it. Know the better half is a human being who engages positively with the environment around him/her. The world includes gender individuals; they choose sexually, so it doesn't imply they deceive you for them. There is a reason they're in close relationship with you. If other people had decided to date them, they would have done it. So, accept the emotions the next time you feel jealous, and adjust the way you talk about the circumstance, and be careful and smart.

2. Calm Down and Stay Vulnerable

Love implies becoming vulnerable. "The more people in your life you love, the weaker you become. What you ought to do is to open your heart to your partner, believe whatever comes along, and remain cool. Sure, it's not easy, but you need to be able to acknowledge what's outside your reach and trust yourself to handle the unknown. You are in a relationship, note because you want to love. This is a decision you make to love your mate and, at the same time, embracing the threats without any doubts or jealousies.

3. Express Your Jealousy in A Soft Way

When you believe your partner is doing something that makes you jealous, you should demonstrate your emotions and speak to them in a rational manner. You may also express it through laughter, tact, or as long as it is polite, explicitly. When you're sarcastic, you might talk about how intensely jealous you are that someone else is paying attention to your partner. Laugh with them when you say so, as it takes off the topic's burden and brings the point across. You should let them realize, while you're polite, that you respect them a lot and that they'll never betray you. So if you're blunt, just remind them you have trust in them, but they can't regulate your feelings and want them to know how you feel.

4. Appreciate Yourself

One of the biggest causes individuals are jealous of is that they have trouble with low self-esteem and anxiety. They seem to believe they're not nice enough, their partner's going to know that, and leave them to someone else. You ought to learn that there's an explanation of why your partner always enjoyed you and got together with you first. When you need a reaffirmation or gratitude, do not hesitate to ask for it (within reason). The next time you feel jealous, note that your companion is with you because your positive attributes make them want to stay with you.

7.5 Other Signs of Healthy Relationship

Comfortable Pace

The relationship moves at a pace that every person finds enjoyable. When you see someone first, it's natural to want to spend a lot of time with them, so it's crucial that both of you are on the same page on how the relationship progresses. You are not stressed or hurried in a successful relationship, in a way that makes you feel frustrated.

Trust

Believe your companion would do nothing to hurt you or break the relationship. Trust falls naturally in a healthy relationship, so you don't have to doubt the motives of the other person, or whether they have your back. They value your privacy and would never evaluate you to show your allegiance.

Honesty

You may be truthful and frank without worrying about how the other individual would react. You will feel that you will express the absolute details about your life and emotions with each other in a good relationship - you should never have to hide anything. They may not like much what you have to tell, but they will react in a considerate way to disappointing news.

Independence

You have freedom beyond the relationship, to be yourself. The other person will support your interests, as well as your interactions with your acquaintances, families, and colleagues. The other person doesn't need to know every part of your life or be involved. Getting liberty means being free to do anything and offering the same right to your partner.

Respect

You respect the values and views of one another, and you appreciate each other for who you are as a human. You feel secure establishing limits and are assured that certain guidelines are accepted by the other person. If you accomplish anything, they cheer for you, support your good work and aspirations, and they love you.

Equality

The relationship seems stable, as both bring the same energy into the relationship's progress. You don't encourage the desires and views of one person to rule, and when you hear each other out and make adjustments if you don't want the same thing. You believe that the desires, expectations, and interests are just as important as those of the other individual. Often you may bring in more than your spouse (money, energy, and emotional support) and vice versa, but the result still seems equal and reasonable.

Kindness

You are compassionate and empathic for each other and provide warmth and support. The other person would do something in a healthy relationship, which they realize would make you happier. Kindness should be a two-way street – it is offered in your relationship, and it is returned. You have concern for the other individual and for the things that matter to them.

Taking Responsibility

Owning your words and your deeds. When you commit a mistake, stop putting blame and should confess it. You should sincerely apologize for having done something wrong and actively seeking to create constructive adjustments to strengthen the relationship. You should take responsibility for the effect your words or actions has, even though your intent was not.

Healthy Conflict

Discuss concerns freely and politely, and confront differences in a non-judgmental way. Conflict is a natural part of every relationship and is anticipated. Everyone has differences, and that's Cool! A healthy dispute acknowledges the underlying cause, and politely fixes it before it escalates into something larger. Nobody should be screaming or belittling during a disagreement.

Fun

Together you love sharing time and bring out the best in one another. A healthy relationship will make you feel pleasant and content. You can let loose, joke together, and be yourself — the relationship isn't about dragging down the mood, but cheering you up. No relationship is 100% fun, but the good days must surely outweigh the bad.

Conclusion:

There are several sources of anxiety, and, depending on the degree of the condition, there are also many different therapies available. The easiest approach to consult a psychiatrist or a psychiatrist is that a combination of therapies can be developed by the therapist or psychologist, ranging from medicine, counseling, methods of self-care, relaxation exercises, etc. By measuring the degree of your fear, they do this and, thus, prescribe the appropriate therapies. Meditation is one of the pillars of rehabilitation at nearly all stages. Meditation is, in no shape or type, intended to be a main anxiety medication. It is a complementary therapy with advantages that reach well beyond what has been demonstrated by medicine and study.

You actually break down harmful thoughts or stimuli, anxiety, and concern by meditation, and you spend all the focus on focusing on intent. You also rely mindfully on the sensations and acknowledge what you can manage and what you cannot.

I hope you think about these meditations if you ever go through a tough time and take a few minutes for yourself. Even if you have just a few minutes, a gentle breathing meditation will help you bring it all into perspective. Know that the longer you exercise, the more your peace of mind gets greater. I hope you've loved practicing fear meditation. Now move ahead to lead your very best life.

CPSIA information can be obtained
at www.ICGtesting.com
Printed in the USA
LVHW060910160821
695353LV00014B/473